Enduring Hope in the Aftermath of War, Loss, and Struggles of Life

Jack Bryant

ISBN 979-8-89526-186-6 (paperback)
ISBN 979-8-89526-187-3 (digital)

Christian Faith Publishing
832 Park Avenue
Meadville, PA 16335
www.christianfaithpublishing.com

Printed in the United States of America

Contents

Acknowledgment

I first acknowledge and give all praise to God. I dedicate this book to the memory and legacy of US Army Sergeant Jack Bryant Jr. I also give glory to God for the opportunity to write about God's grace and His sustaining power in our journey and that He gets the glory for everyone that it may touch. I also want to acknowledge and thank my wife Linda for her support and encouragement in the time and process of writing. Also, to my dear daughters Denie Robinson and Jennifer Souza and life friends Charles Kevin Smith Jr. and his wife Keshon Smith for giving us a beautiful living tribute and legacy by naming their children after Army Sergeant Jack Bryant Jr. whom we affectionately call "Jay" and is what he preferred. We are so grateful and forever thankful to our daughters Denie for naming her daughter Jayla, Jennifer and her husband Travis for naming their daughters Jayda and Paris. He was on R&R in Paris two weeks before going back to Iraq before he was killed, so we have the name "Paris." We are also so grateful to our dear life friends Charles Kevin Smith Jr. and his wife Keshon Smith for naming their oldest son Jayden. The very individual, unique, and lively personalities of these young people give us joy, a wonderful legacy, and, by God's grace, *enduring hope.*

Introduction

This is a message of hope. We go through many things and sometimes horrible things, but in all that we go through, I come to the basic conclusion that even with devastating loss, there is still enduring hope in Jesus Christ. When we look outside of ourselves toward Him, He will masterfully and most assuredly prove Himself faithful in that He will sustain you through life devastations. It is my desire to share hope in light of our loss of Sgt. Jack Bryant Jr. In the midst of when life is not making sense, when we don't understand why, we must understand that there is nothing in life that is beyond God's reach. You may have questioned God, and truth be told, those of us who profess to know Him have questioned Him. I will discuss this more later.

There can be nothing more devastating to a parent than the loss of a child. It does not matter how young or how old the child is or the circumstance. It is difficult to understand and incomprehensible unless you have gone through the same experience. But the contrast that will be consistent throughout this book is that there is enduring hope even in this type of loss. The country has suffered great losses as a result of casualties from the Iraq and Afghanistan wars. Although we are now separated by many years from these conflicts and daily news reports at that time of casualties, understand that within families and fellow veterans, the impact still runs deep affecting spouses, children, parents, uncles, aunts, cousin, and friends. For every service member, multiply that by an untold number of immediate and extended family and close friends. We must remember to embrace all those who feel the impact of loss and embrace them with understanding and compassion. That compassion must also be extended to all veterans of these wars. For many of them, there is a battlefield within that they face with the effects of their experience. There are veterans who bear scars, some seen and unseen. Even now, many years later, we must never forget.

I had early apprehensions of writing on this subject because of fear reliving this life-changing event. The moment we were notified of Jay's death will be forever etched in our hearts. Our daughter-in-law called us at two o' clock on Sunday morning, telling us that Jay was killed when his convoy was attacked with IEDs ("improvised explosive devices") and rocket-propelled grenades. Although we are now separated by many years, we will never forget Jay and our veterans who have served and ultimately given their lives. When it comes to death and loss, the term *closure* gets a lot of attention in our modern day. We desperately want to understand and unravel the mystery of why and how death has occurred—asking many questions within ourselves. All of us must go through and grieve loss. Grieving is not something that you just tough it out for a period and pretend that loss has no effect. This can be at first very shocking, traumatic, and debilitating. Our mourning is the mental, emotional, and physical response to loss. Every individual is different, but generally, everyone responds and then followed by grieving that takes on the form of a journey. Christianity does not give us an easy pill to work through grief. Jesus himself was moved and wept as Martha and her sister Mary mourned the death of their brother Lazarus. The key is that we trust God in the middle of the storms even if our lives as we know it is turned upside down. We work toward and come to a point where we learn how to live with our loved one not being here with us.

It is not possible for parents who have lost children to place them in the far reaches of their minds in the state of forgetfulness. Doing this could have detrimental effects on our emotional and physical well-being. Jay is still with us in our memory and in the history of our family and friends. He was a bit of a jokester and lovable goofball who would always find something funny about every situation, so he is still able to touch our lives. Relearning life's pattern in the absence of him is a journey that we must purpose within ourselves to live in hope. Each family member and friend will travel this life journey a little differently. I believe that grieving is a life journey. It doesn't mean that for my entire life, I am experiencing the debilitating experience of loss.

Over time, by God's grace, He gives us what we need to move forward in hope and strength. We deliberately engage in active memory—the loved one is not shoved into a dark corner. As we deliberately engage in active memory, this allows the heritage of the memory to bring us to positive action in helping others and to allow our lives to be purpose-driven. We continue to have a relationship, although they are physically no longer here with us. We continue to love, cherish their personalities and how they touched us in many ways. John Patton describes relearning this relationship as a life process and not as a static set of predictable stages as some theories of mourning and grieving suggest. He quotes philosopher Thomas Attig as he examines and interprets a longer process of grief as an effort at "relearning the world":

> We lose the presence of the central character or characters in the ongoing stories of our lives. We lose the usual ways of connecting with those who have died, but we learn to continue to love the person of the one who has died, experienced not as something fixed in time or memory but as one who retains the power to move us even as we survive him or her. We continue to love and cherish the stories of a life or lives that have now been completed.[1]

The Christian faith adds another dimension to our world, which is the hope that we shall see him again. This is not positive thinking or some far out fantasy, but by tangible, verifiable evidence in the promise of God. It is by this promise of God's eternal word that allows us to live beyond life circumstances and embrace the endur-

---

[1] John Patton, *Pastoral Care An Essential Guide* (Nashville, Abingdon Press, 2005), 55–56.

ing hope that God brings. My intention is to present a contrasting picture to a life-changing event in my family's history and even the history of our nation. During the height of the Iraq War, the reports of casualties on the news outlets were a daily event. This became a painful reality for many families and as with us found ourselves talking to the local television stations and newspapers about our loss almost immediately. Although this means displaying grief in public, we decided to express what we felt as our witness. The contrasting picture to a difficult episode in our American history is the picture of enduring hope with great loss. This book was a journey over the years since our loss of Jay. Although my focus was on our loss during the Iraq War, I must acknowledge another exceedingly difficult and heart-breaking episode in our American history. At the time of this writing, we are in a coronavirus epidemic that claimed the lives of over two hundred thousand Americans at this point. It is my prayer that the principles of enduring hope will help families who have lost loved ones of all age groups. My dear friends, even in grief, there is joy and peace, and it is obtainable.

I personally could not figure out how it was possible at that time to experience peace when my life was in turmoil. How is this possible? It is possible through the indwelling and sustaining power of the living God. The joy that I speak of is more than a positive attitude or pleasant emotion or delight. It certainly includes those human elements. The joy that God brings rises above circumstances and focuses on the very character of God. His joy gives me assurance that His word is true, and He is faithful. He has proven that He is able to keep us—sustain us when we did not know how we were going to make it. This joy also looks beyond the present world and assures us eternal life in the presence of God with all those that believe. The peace that I speak of is the peace of God. Having a relationship with Jesus Christ means that we have peace with God—meaning, a spiritual connection that did not exist before. My spirit is alive in Him that was once dead in relationship. By having the peace with God, I have the peace of God. The peace of God allows you to have peace and contentment that rise above life's stormy seas. When we put our trust in God through prayer with thanksgiving—making our requests known to Him, the peace of God which surpasses all understanding will guard your hearts and minds through Christ Jesus (Philippians 4:6–7). This is only possible through His indwelling Spirit. This life journey is evolving as we live but always infused with hope. Through the peace of God, this hope becomes enduring. My intent of writing this book is to show how enduring hope is possible and how we can find strength while living under the sovereignty of God.

The Bases of Our Hope

For hope to endure, there must be bases for hope. What are the bases for our hope or what gives us hope—that hope that sustains us day-to-day? First, what is hope? In general, hope is desire accompanied by expectation of or belief in fulfillment in someone or something on which hopes are centered.[2] There must be a reason for hope, or it stands empty and shallow. Hope shapes our attitude and perspective about life. Although hope varies according to human needs in both the Old and New Testaments of the Bible, ultimately, God is the bases of our hope. There is a close correlation between faith and hope, and they are inseparable.

Faith centers on my trust in God, whereas hope is the expectation of what God is going to do. In the New Testament, the Hebrew writer proclaims that "Now faith is the assurance of things hoped for, the conviction of things not seen" (Hebrews 11:1 NASB). The assurance is my confidence in what I am hoping for. The conviction is evidence—what demonstrates my faith. The evidence is how I show my faith in action by what I do. Conviction goes beyond feelings and the human emotional state. Conviction is a product of the human will, which is our volitional ability to choose.

---

2   *Webster's Ninth New Collegiate Dictionary* (Springfield, Massachusetts: Merriam-Webster Inc., 1986), 581.

Although many preachers and teachers use this passage as a definition, the Hebrew writer describes more of what faith does or how faith behaves than a definition. I understand the reason we use this scripture to define faith. Faith requires us to do something. Genuine faith ultimately results in action. Jesus asked the man who was born blind and healed by Jesus, "Do you believe?" The man replied "Lord, I believe," and he worshiped Him (John 9:35–38). His faith was followed by action in worshiping Jesus as the Son of God. Pure worship expresses adoration and veneration—a feeling of awe, respect, and reverence without making petition. Even before he acknowledges to Jesus that he believed, his faith in action testified to the religious leaders the marvelous thing that Jesus has done, and for that reason, they excommunicated him. This word *believe* in the Greek is *pistevo* and is used in the New Testament in this context for entrusting one's well-being to Jesus Christ or saving faith. This is the same word when Jesus responded to the centurion's great faith when he pleaded for his servant to be healed. When Jesus told the centurion, "I will come and heal him," he replied, "but only speak a word, and my servant will be healed." Jesus replied to him, "Go your way; and as you have believed, so let it be done for you" (Matthew 8:13). This man's faith in action sought after Jesus for healing of his servant and desired that Jesus would just speak a word for it to be done. Faith is also expressed in our dependence on God for day-to-day living. Our faith, then, could be defined as believing in God with the predominant idea of trust—entrusting Jesus Christ for salvation, trusting Him for our total human dependence, involving hope for the future and a total commitment to His will. I get the "predominant idea of trust" from Dr. R. C. Sproul's book *What Is Faith*.[3] He describes the Christian life as a pilgrimage, and it begins with God's gift of faith. We entrust Jesus Christ for eternal life and everyday life as we grow and continue to trust our lives to God, His value system, and His word. Faith is a growing process that involves every facet of life and all seasons of life.

---

[3]   R. C. Sproul and Greg Baily, *What Is Faith?* (Crucial Questions Series Book 8), Kindle Locations 32–33).

I Have a Reason for Hope

God gives us the reason for hope so that our hope has substance and is not empty. My goal is to prove that for our hope to be enduring, it must be empowered by three factors: first God is the object of our hope, second, God is sovereign and third, God is trustworthy. Since God is first the object of my hope, I find it necessary to proclaim that God exists. For some, there is only a notional thought of God's existence. There are those who have an agnostic world view, which hold that the existence of the ultimate cause, as God is unknown and unknowable. There are also those who hold an atheistic world view that denies or disbelieves the existence of a supreme being or beings. There are tons of material that defines who God is and how He is defined in Christianity. The most direct and simplest definition that I've come across is "God is the infinite and perfect Spirit in whom all things have their source, support, and end."[4] God proclaims that He exist: "In the beginning God created the heavens and the earth" (Genesis 1:1). Simply put, He is the first cause of the universe. In theology (theology in its most basic definition is the "doctrine of God"), this is the cosmological argument for God's existence. This argument may be stated as this: "Everything begun must have an adequate cause. The universe was begun; therefore, the universe must have an adequate cause for its production."[5] I would offer to those who struggle to see if there is a God to consider simply that the heavens and earth displays His glory. When I consider the vast beauty of the earth and how the heavens are situated for our discovery, it becomes hard to ignore that there is deliberate intelligent design that allows for a perfect condition for sustaining life. This is in collaboration with another theological term that argues for the existence of God called the teleological argument. The teleological argument centers on the fact that the universe is characterized by order and useful arrangement; therefore, the universe has an intelligent and free cause.[6]

---

[4] Henry C. Thiessen, *Lectures in Systematic Theology* (Grand Rapids: William B. Eerdmans Publishing Company, 1997), 25.

[5] Ibid, 27.

[6] Ibid, 28

Consider all the elements required to sustain complex living organisms on the earth. The fact that our atmosphere is clear; that our moon is just the right size and distance from Earth, and that its gravity stabilizes Earth's rotation; that our position in our galaxy is just so; that our sun is its precise mass and composition—all these facts and many more not only are necessary for Earth's habitability but also have been surprisingly crucial to the discovery and measurement of the universe by scientists.[7] The Earth's stabilization ensures relatively temperate seasonal changes suitable for our habitation. As one scientist puts it, "If the moon was not here, we would not be here." There was a total lunar eclipse on August 21, 2017. On parts of the country where they could observe total darkness as the event occurred, there was great excitement, amazement and awe. Some of the people expressed a spiritual experience—a feeling of something beyond themselves. Is it just coincidence that the moon and sun line up perfectly to allow for a total eclipse and allowing for our discovery and scientist to measure the effects? Is this just a fluke as some would suggest? To believe that all around us is a product of chance, all the factors that must come together to sustain life is by accident, that we have hit the cosmic lotto jackpot for all the critical factors to come together is a great leap of faith. Beyond this, to hold the view that we live an insignificant, meaningless, and purposeless existence in the universe puts us at risk of living in hopelessness—particularly when our material world around us and our personal world goes south or turns for the worse. We were created for purpose and our existence has meaning in this universe. Rick Warren in his book *The Purpose Driven Life* makes the point about our existence and purpose:

> You exist only because God wills that you
> exist. You were made by God and for God—and
> until you understand that, life will never make
> sense. It is only in God that we discover our ori-

---

7 Guillermo Gonzalez and Jay W. Richards, *The Privileged Planet* (Washington, DC: Regnery Publishing, 2004), Kindle Location, 110.

gin, our identity, our meaning, our purpose, our significance, and our destiny. Every other path leads to a dead end."[8]

Whether we are willing to accept it or not, it is only in God that we discover our origin, identity, meaning, purpose, significance, and destiny as Rick Warren describes. If these elements are based solely on anything other than God, we will eventually come up void and empty. In the end, no matter how rich or poor we are, you will find what matters in life are our relationship with God, family, and others. With God as the bases of our hope, he gives the ultimate reason for living. When we come to understand and live by the three factors that empower our hope, then our hope is enduring.

The First Factor That Empowers Enduring
Hope: God Is the Object of Our Hope

The writer of the psalms says, "The heavens declare the glory of God; and the firmament shows His handiwork" (Psalm 19:1). "When I consider Your heavens, the work of Your fingers, the moon and the stars, which You have ordained, what is man that You are mindful of him, and the son of man that You visit him?" (Psalm 8). Within every human being there is a consciousness of God. The apostle Paul writes in his letter to the Romans, "For since the creation of the world God's invisible qualities—His eternal power and divine nature have been clearly seen, being understood from what has been made, so that people are without excuse" (Romans 1:20 NIV). God has revealed Himself in our conscious and in nature. There is a moral consciousness within every person—a sense of moral law that can only be given by a law giver and not as a product of evolution or natural extinction.

In general, this is considered the moral argument for the existence of God. As human beings, we have the volitional ability to

---

[8] Rick Warren, *The Purpose Driven Life: What On Earth Am I Here For?* (Grand Rapids, Zondervan, 2012), 23.

choose what to believe, how to act on what we believe and who or what we choose to worship. The intent is not to exhaust the arguments for the existence of God but to give what is first in the bases of our hope. God as the object of our hope is the first factor that empowers enduring hope. When we look deeply within ourselves, we will find flaws and imperfections. When our hope is totally based on human ability and the ability of others, we will eventually come up short. I love my wife, children, and grandchildren; but it is not possible for them or another human being to fulfill all my hope. Total fulfillment and completion in life can only come from God. This does not mean we neglect family and friends. In fact, when God is first, and He is the object of our hope we put family first because we follow His standard for living and moral principles by His word. Surely, God will use friends, family, and fellow church members to help in a time of need; but there are limitations to the human capacity to fulfill all our needs. We get frustrated and perplexed when promises are unmet and when people fail us. Many of us are strong individuals, but we sometimes fail ourselves. Even the apostle Paul who wrote most of the New Testament had internal struggles. He said,

> I love God's law with all my heart. But there is another power within me that is at war with my mind. This power makes me a slave to the sin that is still within me. Oh, what a miserable person I am! Who will free me from this life that is dominated by sin and death? Thank God! The answer is in Jesus Christ our Lord. (Romans 7:22–25 NLT)

As a person who knows God through a personal relationship with Jesus Christ, there are internal personal struggles and shortcomings that I face and many of us face. As the apostle Paul concluded that the answer is in Jesus Christ our Lord, we must come to the same conclusion. Not only in the New Testament but the Old Testament writers also understood firmly that God is the object of our hope.

The psalmist said, "For You are my hope, O Lord God; You are my trust from my youth" (Psalm 71:5). Considering the condition of human frailty, there must be a basis for hope that is external to ourselves. Therefore, our enduring hope is first and foremost based on God as the object of our hope.

The Second Factor That Empowers
Enduring Hope: God Is Sovereign

So since God is first the object of our hope, the second factor that empowers enduring hope is God is sovereign. The sovereignty of God is a theological term that refers to the unlimited power of God Who has sovereign control over the affairs of nature and history. Here is where it gets ugly, and we begin to run into difficulty and where I personally had to struggle through. But with God as the object of our hope, there is resolution. We see from the definition of this term that God is in control and has authority of all things, yet there is great suffering. Human suffering is defined broadly as agony, affliction, distress, intense pain, or sorrow.[9] We are assured of His sovereignty by what He says in scripture. Jesus is described as the image of the invisible God, the firstborn over all creation—meaning He holds preeminence.

> For by Him all things were created that are
> in heaven and that are on earth, visible and invis-
> ible, whether thrones or dominions or principal-
> ities or powers. All things were created through
> Him and for Him and He is before all things, and
> in Him all things consist. (Colossians 1:16–17)

God is one God revealed in three persons—God the Father, God the Son, and God the Holy Spirit. Jesus as the second person in the Godhead proclaims that all authority has been given to Him in

---

9   Herbert Lockyer Sr., et al., eds., *Nelson's Illustrated Bible Dictionary* (Nashville: Thomas Nelson Publishers, 1986), 1015.

heaven and in earth, yet with this assurance, we struggle. We struggle to see terrible things happen to the innocent in our environment. At the time of the drafting this chapter, there was a high school mass shouting in Parkland, Florida, on February 14, 2018, where seventeen persons, most of them teenage students, were murdered at the hands of another student. The *New York Times* reported around this time frame that the numbers of mass shootings are mind-numbing. More than 430 people have been shot in 273 school attacks since the one at Sandy Hook Elementary School in 2012. This is just within the schools—not counting all the other horrible events of mass shootings within the United States and other categories of human suffering. At this point, it is probably difficult to see how the sovereignty of God is one of the factors that empowers enduring hope. It is extremely difficult to see how events and life circumstances work according to God's plan and purpose when suffering is a part of the human life journey. We live in a fallen sin condition with the whole of creation subject to the curse, but as in the human condition, creation also eagerly waits for the revealing of the sons of God when the curse is lifted, and God restores creation as it was in the beginning (Romans 8:18–19). What cursed the beginning was sin by Adam as the corporate agent for humanity, so as human beings, we are subject to the consequences of sin. In other words, we all have inherited a sin nature because of Adam's sin. With the inherited sin nature is the reality of a personal enemy called Satan. But we are assured by the obedience of Jesus Christ in giving His life for us, many will be made righteous. With the righteousness of God, there is His power toward us who believe which God worked in Christ when He raised Him from the dead and seated Him at His right hand in heavenly places.

"Jesus Christ is far above all principalities and power and might and dominion, and every name that is named, not only in this age but also in that which is to come" (Ephesians 1:20–21).

We have a powerful enemy, but Jesus proclaims all authority has been given to Him in heaven and on earth. The Bible also proclaims that He who is in you is greater than he who is in the world (1 John 4:4). This includes Satan and his demons. Even with this assurance, the Bible describes the whole of creation groans and suffers the pains as in childbirth because of the consequence of sin (Romans 8:22). Theology does not provide easy answers to suffering while serving under God's sovereign rule. In the biblical story of Job, God describes him as "blameless and an upright man, one who fears God and shuns evil," yet Job was afflicted with suffering under God's sovereign rule and His purpose. If I had to put this in a biblical model, it would be this: The testing of faith produces perseverance and from perseverance proven character and from proven character hope. Hope brings underlining comfort as we look forward to Jesus who is the author and the finisher of our faith (Hebrews 12:1–2). Even in the Old Testament, the old saints looked forward to the promises of God. This brings us hope because when we trust Him; the experience of His faithfulness brings hope. Even in human relationships when they are long-lasting, consistently faithful, and committed, they bring us comfort. Jesus promised that He is with us always. He promised the Holy Spirit, "the Spirit of truth whom the world cannot receive but will live with us and in us. He said that I will not leave you as orphans; I will come to you" (John 14:17–18). We can only look to Jesus in hope if there is a personal relationship with Him and that we allow ourselves to be governed by the indwelling Holy Spirit to do His will amid suffering. We must choose to respond to the Holy Spirit who will teach us and bring His word to remembrance as we study and meditate on it as Jesus promised in John 14:26. For the Word of God is alive and active—it judges the thoughts and attitudes of the heart. If we abide in His word, His word becomes a part of us. As the psalmist says, "Your word is a lamp for my feet, a light on my path" (Psalm 119:105). Only then can all things work together for our good with God's ultimate objective for us to be conformed to the image of Jesus Christ (2 Corinthians 3:18). Absent a relationship with Jesus Christ, we are spiritually dead and will not be able to respond to the ministry work of the Holy Spirit to our souls in a difficult time of suffering. The choice is ours to yield our lives to Jesus Christ or determine to make a recommitment to Him if we have fallen away.

Dumbfounded by Suffering

As a preacher and teacher, I can reason with theology and scripture to gather how to deal with suffering, but the life journey is difficult, and sometimes, we are just dumbfounded or just speechless by what happens to us. The loss of a loved one and especially the loss of our only son Jay in Iraq was an unnatural rendering of the heart. This is unnatural because sin and death had entered our human experience. In this we get perplexed, confused, and dumbfounded, so I must defer to God's wisdom and not my own understanding. We will not fully comprehend the reasons why tragic events occur in life. The why question is one that many of us ask, but this is one of the most difficult questions to contend with in life. Let me give a perspective from Jesus's own words. In the beginning of this chapter, I mention the man born blind to illustrate his faith in action. In the Gospel according to John's chapter 9, it begins an interesting story with Jesus and His disciples. Jesus saw a man who was born blind from birth. This man was most likely begging on the roadside. The disciples had the same observation, and they said, "Rabbi, who sinned, this man or his parents, that he was born blind?" This was a false belief that this man's sin had caused his blindness. Old Testament scripture demonstrates that life begins at conception (Psalm 139:13–16; Jeremiah 1:5). It is unconceivable that an unborn child could sin. Their question comes from the false perspective that his disabilities were caused by his sin and his parents' sin. Jesus's answer to the question was not what they expected. Jesus said, "Neither this man nor his parents sinned, but that the works of God should be revealed in him." The disciples were looking for a reason for this man's suffering. This man's life during this time meant a life of poverty with no means of support. Jesus shifted their attention away from the cause to purpose. The fact is this man was born blind of no fault of his own. Jesus did not provide a reason for his suffering but only that in this journey of life, the works of God should be revealed in us even in suffering. God's glory was manifested in this man being healed in this story, but the wider purpose is God's divine plan. Dr. J. Lyle Story writes this perspective on Jesus's answer:

> Jesus' answer liberates us from obsession with theory and with endless analysis of why bad things happen. His word asks us to be sensitive to the ways in which God may move amidst the broken conditions in life that we face every day. Until now, the man has been living a purpose-less existence; he lives as a burden to others. But Jesus says that this man born blind is to become a sign of God's majesty and power.[10]

Our goal should not be to speculate on the reasons why we suffer, but to look to the divine purpose at work in brokenness. We may not see this in the immediate or even in years, but we trust in the one who is able to keep us from stumbling. As the writer of Jude in the New Testament says, "To God our Savior Who alone is wise."

Seek After Him and Allow Access

The New Testament writer James in his letter said, "If any of you lacks wisdom, let him ask of God, who gives to all liberally and without reproach, and it will be given to him" (James 1:5). I am no giant of the faith but a witness of what God can do. Although I was aware of mourning and grieving and the human effects, there were exceedingly difficult moments where I could not see my way amid this experience of loss. I had moments of feeling perplexed, confused, and overwhelmed. Suffering can paralyze us figuratively speaking in our mental and emotional state. What stops us from realizing the sovereignty of God is an unwillingness to totally submit to Him while we are hurting. God being who He is will not force His will on us but allow

---

[10] J. Lyle Story, *Jesus and the Issue of Suffering* (Virginia Beach: Regent University, 2008), 5.

us to choose who to follow. Sometimes it seems that God is silent when we are suffering, but His word speaks loudly.

"Come to Me, all you who labor and are heavy laden, and I will give you rest." (Matthew 11:28)

"Draw near to God and He will draw near to you." (James 4:8)

For the Holy Spirit to minister to our souls through His word, we must give Him access to every dark room and dark corner of our lives. There is help in our dreadful time of need. You may be angry in grief and experiencing profound sadness, but by the act of your human will allow Him access to the dark place. The dark place can represent the most dreadful and difficult circumstance we find ourselves in life. This certainly can amount to our suffering. The loneliness of suffering comes when we don't allow Jesus into the dark place, and we find ourselves in hopelessness. We allow Him access by acknowledging Him in prayer. God can handle your questions, your anger, your anguish, and everything that is going on inside. After all, He made you—who knows you best? Is it okay to question God? In the psalms, we find David and other writers expressing the full range of human emotion in times of stress and anxieties and yes questioning God. Consider Psalm 13 where David begins with questions: "How long, O Lord? Will You forget me forever? How long will You hide Your face from me? How long shall I take counsel in my soul, Having sorrow in my heart daily? How long will my enemy be exalted over me?" (Psalm 13:1–2).

Verses 1 and 2 expresses the anxieties we feel that God is silent and does not hear us. When you look at the end of this psalm, we observe a shift in his focus from the enemy that's causing such despair to God in whom David is putting his trust. David recognizes God's mercy that causes his heart to rejoice because God has dealt bountifully with him: "But I have trusted in Your mercy; My heart shall rejoice in Your salvation. I will sing to the Lord, because He has dealt bountifully with me" (Psalm 13:5–6).

How is this possible? When we open ourselves to God even in anger and despair, He brings us to where we need to be. In David's case, it was reminding him that He has dealt with Him bountifully or treated well. By limiting the depth of communication with God, we become shallow in our relationship with Him. Let His word guide you into deeper and authentic communication with Him. By doing this, we allow the Holy Spirit to minister to our souls.

The Bible encourages us to pray, "Let your request be made known to God" (Philippians 4:6b). But it is our responsibility to initiate and make the connection. When you allow Him access, you can tap into His sustaining power. Jesus prayed while in agony before being betrayed by one of His disciples named Judas. Jesus prayed in Luke 22:42 to God the Father, saying, "Father, if it is Your will, take this cup away from Me; nevertheless, not My will, but Yours, be done." In the next verse, an angel appeared to Him from heaven, strengthening Him. As in the example with Jesus's life, even in agony, there is strengthening and sustaining power through the connection of prayer. God may not take you out of the circumstance you are in, but He will give you what you need to go through it. Jesus requested in His prayer if it be possible for this cup—the suffering that He knew was ahead of Him to be taken away. But He knew it was the Father's will for Him to go through. Waiting for the pain to go away or for there to be a more convenient time with God is not the right time. My encouragement to you is make connection while you are amid pain and anguish.

One of the traps of the enemy is to get you isolated and in a state of hopelessness. Do not allow the pain of the present time to stop you from connecting to the very power source that will help you. You can have the most powerful computer industry can produce but absent of the power source by way of its battery or the AC outlet, the powerful computer with the most advanced processing technology is dead. By the power of the Holy Spirit, Jesus can lift you up while you are in a dreadful dark place. While in the dark place, the peace of God is possible when we allow Him access. The connection is made in faith—yes, even give thanksgiving when you pray. The benefit is the peace of God that goes beyond human understanding will guard your hearts and minds like a soldier standing guard, so we do not lose it. Continue to seek after Him and allow access.

Jesus: A Man Acquainted with Grief

Jesus can relate because He has been there before in a dark place in history while suffering through the process of the most dreadful forms of execution in human history—the ancient Roman death through crucifixion. There were two condemned thieves being crucified with Jesus. When one of the thieves made the choice to mock Him and ridicule, the other thief recognized Him for who He is and requested that Jesus remember him when He come into His kingdom. Jesus replied, "Assuredly, I say to you, today you will be with Me in Paradise." The condemned thief was not only assured eternal life in paradise with Jesus Christ forever but was assured that Jesus was already there with him in the darkest place in life. The condemned thief made the choice to connect with Jesus Christ, and He met him where he was in that dreadful dark place. How profound that even in a dark place, Jesus was ministering to someone else. It is possible that while there is great sadness and heaviness, there is strength when we witness His light. People would ask us, "How are you and your wife doing?" Or they would say, "We don't know how you all are making it." I often would tell them it is only through our relationship with Jesus Christ that we are making it. This is regardless of who was asking the question.

Another observation as Jesus was suffering was that he cried out to God. Recorded in Mark 15:34 and Matthew 27:46, He said, "My God, My God, why have You forsaken Me?" This was not a frivolous, hopeless, desperate cry for help but a phrase that carries significance for us that indicated his awareness of God's hand in his suffering. Jesus was quoting Psalm 22:1. In his humanity, He expressed the feeling of abandonment and distance from God as David did in this first verse. Psalm 22 is unique in that it prophetically points toward the crucifixion of Jesus as David details the mocking, ridicule (Psalm

22:6–7) pain, and opposition (Psalm 22:14–18)—all done to an innocent man. Jesus felt the heavy weight that was placed upon Him. The Bible says, "For He made Him who knew no sin to be sin for us, that we might become the righteousness of God" (2 Corinthians 5:21). This is not just for the few, but for the whole world; "And He Himself is the propitiation for our sins, and not for ours only, but also for the whole world" (1 John 2:2). The word *propitiation* refers to Jesus Christ atoning death for our sins which brings us into fellowship with God. Jesus crying out to God in His word during unimaginable pain and suffering is a significant observation for all of us. As with our prayer to God that provides strengthening and sustaining power through connecting to the power source, praying in His word and meditating on His word is an equal sustaining factor.

Psalm 119:50 says, "This is my comfort in my affliction, that Your word has revived me" (NASB). The word *revived* is a verb and it means to live, have life, remain alive, or sustain life. God's Word will keep you and sustain you amid suffering. I would suggest that the study of and meditation on God's Word be a part of everyday life so when life trouble comes, there is a foundation that is laid, and you stand on it. In Avery T. Willis Jr.'s book *Master Life*, he describes the benefits of remaining in the Word:

> Spending time in the Word will allow you to deal with the circumstances of life that come your way. Christians are not exempt from difficulties but remaining in His Word cultivates a relationship with Christ in which you can successfully weather those storms. When you have a relationship with Christ, His Spirit uses the scripture as the source of guidance and strength.[11]

The passion of Jesus Christ included the suffering and agony of the cross; however, He never lost sight of God's word—He never

---

[11] Avery T. Willis Jr., *Master Life, Developing a Rich Personal Relationship with the Master* (Nashville, Broadman & Holman Publishers, 1998), 18.

wavered from who God is and His relationship. What His relationship showed us is that we should never lose sight of God's Word no matter how dreadful the pain and suffering. Believe what He said and stand on His eternal truth. Remember Jesus has been there in a dark place and understand fully our human condition. That's not the end of the story. Jesus is risen! He voluntarily gave up His life on the cross, but on the third day He arose. We serve a God that is not a dead hope but a living hope. There is no dark place unreachable by Him. An old gospel song by the William Sisters said, "Jesus will pick you up, if He has to reach way down." For many of us, He must reach way down, but because God is sovereign, there is no place—no dark place that is unreachable by Him.

Liberation Through the God Who Knows Me

In my journey, I encountered Psalm 139, which directly speaks of His sovereignty over our human existence. What this psalm has revealed to me is God see my life and Jay's life in its entirety from the beginning and the ending all at the same time. The theme of Psalm 139 is God's perfect knowledge of man and sovereignty over our affairs. I often use portions of this psalm as part of my worship before prayer because King David's total worship is directed toward God. What's more important is the level of intimate knowledge that God has of me, Jay, and all of us in our earliest forms of life. The first six verses speak of God's knowledge of my total person including personality, thoughts, and all the unique characteristics that makes us individuals.

> O Lord, You have searched me and known me. You know my sitting down and my rising up; You understand my thought afar off. You comprehend my path and my lying down, And are acquainted with all my ways. For there is not a word on my tongue, But behold, O Lord, You know it altogether. You have hedged me behind and before, And laid Your hand upon me. Such

knowledge is too wonderful for me; It is high, I
cannot attain it. (Psalm 139:1–6)

David is at awe with God's omniscience—that is, His all-knowing and superior knowledge and wisdom. As indicated in the introduction, we respond to grieving differently in this life journey, but God comprehends our individual uniqueness and personal characteristics. We can be confident that we are not invisible to Him, for He fully comprehends our path—the journey before us and the end of our life's journey. He is intimately familiar with all our ways to include what others may find oddball, God rather sees and values the total person. Jesus proclaimed in Matthew 10:30, "But the very hairs of your head are all numbered." Given God's all-knowing of us, David said, "Such knowledge is too wonderful for me," or in other words, incomprehensible; it is extraordinary. He said in verse 6, "It is high, I cannot attain it." The word *high* in this verse is a verb, and in the Hebrew, it means "to be exalted of God." God's knowledge of us is not something to be taken unfair advantage of or for evil intent on us, but as a father who is aware of his children's uniqueness uses the knowledge for good. As a father of three, I realize that each child is different and responds differently to parenting. Although we strive to be consistent in our love and commitment toward our children, we realize the unique personhood of each child. God knows this about us as well and comprehends us more than we can imagine.

I tried to comprehend God as a young army officer going through a communications course at Fort Gordon, Georgia. In an open field during a break in training, I was alone waiting for fellow students to return from a task. I decided to lay down on a wooden platform used by instructors to conduct physical exercises and gazed at the clear blue Georgia sky. There were no clouds or any other objects in my field of vision—just the sky. In my twenty-two-year-old mind, I tried to comprehend God. I immediately felt overwhelmed and had to get up. I do not know whether this was a spiritual experience or the fact that in my field of vision there was nothing but blue sky, but the feeling was too overwhelming, and I had to get up. What came to my mind even then is that our human finite minds are not able to comprehend God. The Old Testament prophet Isaiah speaks about God's thoughts and His ways: "For my thoughts are not your thoughts, Nor are your ways My ways, says the Lord. For as the heavens are higher than the earth, So are My ways higher than your ways, And My thoughts than your thoughts" (Isaiah 55:8–9).

There will be times when we will not comprehend why things happen in life, but as I stated previously, His word is what will sustain us in life when it is hard to understand. God reveals Himself through revelation of His word, and through Jesus Christ, we come to know Him in an intimate way. This not a vague notion of God, not the man upstairs, not a general way but in an intimate way. So I continue to reflect on Psalm 139—no one knows me or you better.

> Where can I go from Your Spirit? Or where can I flee from Your presence? If I ascend into heaven, You are there; If I make my bed in hell, behold, You are there. If I take the wings of the morning, And dwell in the uttermost parts of the sea, Even there Your hand shall lead me, And Your right hand shall hold me. If I say, "Surely the darkness shall fall on me," Even the night shall be light about me; Indeed, the darkness shall not hide from You, But the night shines as the day; The darkness and the light are both alike to You. (Psalm 139:7–12)

David presents a rhetorical question that expects the answer "nowhere." Nowhere can we go from His Spirit. The extreme conditional situations that the psalmist presents is no match for God—not in hell or even in the uttermost parts of the sea. Through the journey of life, God leads us, and while in the thick of life, His right hand shall hold us. In a biblical sense, God's right hand is the hand of power—namely, the power of God. The power of God is what holds you together. Life experiences such as loss of a loved one takes you to the edge, and it won't take much to topple you over. But wherever the edge of life that you find yourself, even there, His hand shall lead you and His right hand shall hold you together. In other words, you are not walking in the hardest episodes of life alone. Remember, Jesus will meet you where you are and enable you to move forward. God will lead us in the right direction and, by His power, holds us in assurance even in the darkest of night. So we live our lives confidently for God knowing that not only is there nowhere we can go from His Spirit but He also created and uniquely crafted us for His purpose as verses 13 through 16 reflects.

> For You formed my inward parts; You covered me in my mother's womb I will praise You, for I am fearfully and wonderfully made; Marvelous are Your works, And that my soul knows very well. My frame was not hidden from You, When I was made in secret, And skillfully wrought in the lowest parts of the earth. Your eyes saw my substance, being yet unformed. And in Your book they all were written, The days fashioned for me, When as yet there were none of them. (Psalm 139:13–16)

Verses 13 through 16 is unique in that it focusses attention to God's involvement while we are in our mother's womb. These verses have a lot to say about the abortion issue of our modern day. David acknowledges God's deliberate involvement in the earliest stages of life, and ultimately, it is His sovereign will when life begins and when it ends. We should all know that we are valued and a wonderful creation of God. David used the word *wrought* in verse 15, and in Hebrew, the word is *raqam*. The word is associated with the skilled craftmanship of an embroiderer commonly used to design the ephod, which was worn by the high priest made of fine linen interwoven with some threads of pure gold and other threads that were blue, purple, and scarlet in color.[12] The word generally means

---

[12] Herbert Lockyer Sr., et al., eds., *Nelson's Illustrated Bible Dictionary* (Nashville: Thomas Nelson Publishers, 1986), 346.

to fabricate—embroiderer, needlework, and to skillfully work. In our modern day, we may not think much about an embroiderer because this is done by machine, but in this context, the work is by hand and signifies the careful, skillful, and meticulous attention to detail that God put into the design of human life in its earliest form. In the earliest form of life in our mother's womb, we receive God's deliberate craftsmanship of individual design unique to our being in the physical and mental makeup, personality, and gifts. The embroiderer as a work of many colors signifies royalty and significance. Human life in its earliest form is royal and precious in the sight of God.

God sees my life and your life in its entirety. The word *fashioned* in verse 16 has reference to shape as with a potter. It also has reference to predestined or preordained. What is evident in this psalm is my life and my son's life doesn't belong to me; it all belongs to God. To think of the days ordained for us perhaps presents anxiety for some of us, but we live in time and space and only see in part God's total plan. Our trust is in His plan for our life because He has already proven that He is the creator, and like the manufacturer of the most advanced information system or intricate machinery, He is perfectly aware of the inner workings of our parts—the physical, mental, and individual personalities. I trust God that my son's life is precious in His sight, and He has fashioned his days according to His will and I will continue to trust Him.

This psalm of David speaks to my heart. The deliberate design and intricate crafting of us as human beings confirm who we belong to. The passing of our loves ones in Jesus Christ means He is receiving what already belongs to Him. Absent of knowing God, this is an empty statement, but knowing Him we can find comfort because of God's perfect knowledge of us. Even being armed with the knowledge of His word, our faith fails and is tempted with hopelessness. It is in these moments where the grace of God carries us in our weakness and failures. The apostle Paul said, "And He said to me My grace is sufficient for you, My strength is made perfect in weakness" (2 Corinthians 12:9). It is in His strength that we must come to rely upon to carry us through each step in this process. The Gospel artist

Travis Green sings a song titled "Made A Way." In the course of his song, he proclaims, "When our backs were against the wall and it looked as if it was over, you made a way. And we're standing here Only because you made a way." The loss is still difficult; but I have no doubt in my heart that God is sovereign, He is in control, and He is trustworthy.

The Third Factor That Empowers Enduring Hope: God Is Trustworthy

Enduring hope from the beginning of this discussion is empowered by God as first the object of our hope; second, God is sovereign; and third, God is trustworthy. We put our trust in many things including our intellect, wealth, people, social status, and things. When I turn the ignition in my car or push a button, I trust most of the time that the engine will start. So what exactly is the relationship of trust and faith? I mention earlier that "faith is believing in God with the predominant idea of trust—entrusting Jesus Christ for salvation, trusting Him for our total human dependence, involving hope for the future and total commitment to His will." From how I define faith, they are very much integrated and not easily separated into components. Again, I quote the great teacher and theologian R. C. Sproul who speaks of the close correlation of faith and trust: "In a real sense, hope is faith looking forward. The word faith carries a strong element of trust. If my hope is based on something God has said will happen in the future, the hope I have for that future promise finds its substance from my trust and confidence in the One making the promise."[13]

Other authors will have different expressions of faith and trust, but one thing is for sure: We must have confidence in Him when faith is fleeting and hope for the future feels lost. When faith feels stripped down to the bare surface of our being, we must be determined to trust Him. The Old Testament gave exhortations to trust

---

[13] R.C. Sproul and Greg Bailey, *What Is Faith?* (Crucial Questions Series Book 8), Kindle Locations 32–34).

God when He is the object of trust. David certainly gave encouragement in trusting God:

> Blessed is that man who makes the Lord his trust. (Psalm 40:4)

> Trust in Him at all times, you people; Pour out your heart before him; God is a refuge for us. (Psalm 62:8)

> Offer the sacrifices of righteousness, And put your trust in the Lord. (Psalm 4:5)

Also, the prophet Jeremiah said, "Blessed is the man who trust in the Lord and whose hope is the Lord" (Jeremiah 17:7). In the Old Testament, they had faith in God just as we do. They look forward to the promises of Jesus Christ, whereas for us, the work of Jesus Christ has been fulfilled, and our faith is inclusive of entrusting Him for salvation. As with our faith, the Old Testament saints trusted God and hoped in His promises. We may ask the question, why should God be trusted? Consider just a few of His attributes that are far above human attributes and how scripture confirms who He is. Scripture says, "God is not man, so he does not lie. He is not human, so He does not change his mind" (Numbers 23:19). I am surely glad God is not man who can be unpredictable, subject to human frailty, insecurities, and depravity. This gives me comfort in a God who is trustworthy.

First, God is unchanging! "Every good gift and every perfect gift is from above, and comes down from the Father of lights, with whom there is no variation or shadow of turning" (James 1:17). In other words, He does not change like shifting shadows. Scripture declares that He remains the same: "For I am the Lord, I do not change" (Malachi 3:6). The Hebrew writer in the New Testament contrast the temporary nature of the world with the unchanging nature of God:

> You, Lord, in the beginning laid the foundation of the earth, and the heavens are the work of Your hands. They will perish, but You remain; and they will grow old like a garment; Like a cloak You will fold them up, and they will be changed. But You are the same, and Your years will not fail. (Hebrews 1:10–12)

The theological term is called the *immutability* of God. The immutability of God does not mean that He will not use different methods in working with us in our relationship with Him. God is active in relationship with us throughout our growth process, and we can be assured His promises to us remains the same. Second, God is all-knowing! He is infinite in knowledge that includes all there is about us—our thoughts and actions in the future. As we discovered in Psalm 139, God is all-knowing of our human existence. "You understand my thought afar off, For there is not a word on my tongue, but behold, O Lord You know it all together" (Psalm 139:2, 4). As God's creations, we are not robots, but created in His image with an active will and ability to make decisions. With God's infinite knowledge of human beings and the world around us, we are not void of responsibilities and are accountability to our decisions. The theological term for God all-knowing attribute is called omniscience. The theologian Henry Thiessen describes this attribute: "He knows himself and all other things perfectly from all eternity, whether they be actual or merely possible, whether they be past, present, or future. He knows things immediately, simultaneously, exhaustively, and truly."[14]

So why should all this matter to me? It matters because I am assured that He understands my human condition and circumstances. When I call on Him, He hears me regardless of how bad I am feeling

---

[14] Henry C. Thiessen, *Lectures in Systematic Theology* (Grand Rapids: William B. Eerdmans Publishing Company, 1997), 81.

or how low I am thinking of myself. When I call His name, I know that He will answer. The answer may not come in when I want it, but because He knows me, the answer is in His perfect time. I trust that this attribute is true because His word is true. The omnipresence of God further proves His omniscience: "The eyes of the Lord are in every place, keeping watch on the evil and the good" (Proverbs 15:3). The prophet Jeremiah proclaims God omnipresence: "Am I a God near at hand, says the Lord, And not a God afar off? Can anyone hide himself in secret places, So I shall not see him? Says the Lord; Do I not fill heaven and earth? Says the Lord" (Jeremiah 23:23–24).

Because I trust that God is who He says He is, this is like an anchor to my soul. I don't fear His all-knowing but take comfort that my soul is anchored in God, and He will not let me go. Although He knows every ugly thought, fault, and other hang-ups, He loves me despite me. We may dislike or hate a person because of what we know in part, but God knows it all and He loves me and He loves you. In this relationship with Jesus, the Holy Spirit partners with God to minister to our souls. "Now He who searches the hearts knows what the mind of the Spirit is, because He makes intercession for the saints according to the will of God" (Romans 8:27). God, in His omniscience, searches the heart, which is figuratively speaking of the soul or mind and the Holy Spirit intercedes to God on our behalf. Because we do not know what we should pray for as we ought, when I am struggling to articulate to God because of emotional and physical pain, the Holy Spirit understands and articulates my needs to God the Father. God is trustworthy because of who He is. His word is proven true, and He also proves Himself in personal experience.

In one of my adult Bible classes, a student made a wonderful observation as we were studying Romans chapter 15. In this prayer in verse 13, the apostle Paul was making to the first-century church at Rome: "Now may the God of hope fill you with all joy and peace in believing, that you may abound in hope by the power of the Holy Spirit." The observation was that some people would grab hold of only a glimmer of hope because that is all they know after experiencing absolute hopelessness. Specifically, people are coming to the border between the United States and Mexico at the time of this writing for the most part with the hope of finding a better life. This is with the risk of being detained or having their children separated from them. For them, the glimmer of hope in the United States is better than the hopelessness they are fleeing.

The observation is that there is no comparison to the hope that God gives us. For His hope not only sustains and keeps us as we go through in our present life but for all eternality. This prayer in the apostle Paul's teaching represents a benediction as he begins to conclude this section of his letter. The hope that he is describing is not a tentative wish that may or may not come true. Christian hope is an assured expectation based on the promises of God. God gives us enduring hope. By the evidence of God's Word and personal experience, our enduring hope is empowered by three factors: first, God is the object of our hope; second, God is sovereign; and third, God is trustworthy. The next chapter, "Faith on Thin Ice," will show how God is worthy of our trust.

Faith on Thin Ice

I borrowed from this popular idiom or expression that generally means someone doing something risky that could have serious consequences. Faith on thin ice, in this presentation, means we all have challenges and gaps in faith and will feel at any moment things will fall apart into disaster. We may at times feel like we are at risk of falling through thin ice. Once fallen through, the conditions are deadly, and chances of getting out on your own are minimal. You may ask the question, how can you feel this way when considering God's perspective about faith? Scripture says, "Without faith, it is impossible to please God" (Hebrews11:6). The apostle Paul highlights this further by stating, "The just shall live by faith" (Romans 1:17). Those of us who have union with God through Jesus Christ are righteous in God's sight. When God sees us, He sees the righteousness of Christ. This is a foreign righteousness that none of us earned because it is a gift to all those who believe in Jesus Christ. Through the righteous act of Jesus Christ, the gift came to all men, resulting in justification of life (Romans 5:18). Simply put, justification is the act of God whereby he declares righteous those of us who believes in Jesus Christ. So with all this assurance by His eternal word, we who are just in God's eyes may still come to a breaking point while struggling in this journey.

There are moments when we are messed up and wondering how things are going to turn out. There are moments when we allow fear to be dominant and feel we are going to fall. Let us relook at how I defined *faith*: "Believing in God with the predominant idea of trust—entrusting Jesus Christ for salvation, trusting Him for our total human dependence, involving hope for the future and a total commitment to His will." It would not be very practical to take this definition and live it out in its totality all at once. There are stages in life as we first come into a relationship with Jesus Christ. There is first saving faith for salvation, and as we grow, we continue to trust Him in every season of life as He shapes and mold us according to His purpose. God uses what we call sanctification, which is the process of setting us apart and preparing us in fulfilling His purpose for us to be more like Jesus Christ. In this, we learn to trust and commit our lives to His will. There are portions of this definition that may come into importance depending on the circumstances of life. In our definition of faith, there is a strong element of trust. For me, there were moments when trusting in God was moment by moment and in the right now. A glimmer of hope may be in the back of my mind, but my circumstance brought me to a place where all I knew to do was cry out, "LORD, I NEED YOU!" An old Rev. James Cleveland gospel song simply says, "Lord, do it." One of the most difficult moments in working through the loss of a loved one is the first annual day, which could be a birthday, holiday, or other events that remind you the loved one is no longer here. For me, it was Christmas 2004.

The difficult moment was when my wife Linda wanted me to help the girls with putting together Christmas toys for the grandsons. At that time, our oldest grandson DeJuan was five and Jay's son Keshawn Bryant just turned three. The most dreadful thought was reliving putting together Jay's toys, his Tonka trucks, and big wheels (1980s toy). The thought was so dreadful that I wanted all the activities of Christmas to quickly pass and get it over with. I wanted this night to pass quickly. Typically, preparing the toys in our family is in the early hours of the morning. I got up feeling like I weighed a ton and slowly made my way to the hallway leading to the steps downstairs. As I started downstairs, my thought was I am going to lose my mind, lose control of everything. I could not see how to face life at this moment. I am on thin ice and at any moment will fall through. On the way downstairs, I just prayed for less than ten seconds for the Lord to help me. The prayer was just that "LORD, HELP ME!" I got downstairs and sat down like a rock on my familiar blue chair. As I sat thinking I am right now good for nothing, I observed an amazing sight. The girls, my two daughters, Denie, Jennifer, and our daughter in-law Kiona were busy like Santa elves putting together the toys, arranging things, organizing all the things around the Christmas tree. They ignored me!

The most amazing sight was watching my youngest daughter Jennifer with a screwdriver in one hand and instructions in the other putting together an electronic basketball game with a score board and hoop. It required assembly. Fast-forward for a moment, Jennifer is now a married woman and mother of three. I am confident there has not been any further toy assemblies since then, so this was divine intervention. As I sat there like a big heavy rock, God encouraged me through some unlikely means and answered my desperate less than ten second prayer request. The only thing the girls wanted me to do was to take the trash away. That I was able to handle.

This episode may not have seemed big, but it was a desperate crisis in my mind that I did not see a way out of. God intervened on my behalf through unexpected and unusual means. I am reminded of how God delivered others by unusual and unexpected means. In the book of Acts chapter 27 begins an amazing journey in the apostle Paul's life. The Jewish leaders had him arrested by the Roman author-ities, but the legality of the charges was questionable. The apostle Paul appealed to Caesar to hear his case. His appeal placed him on a first-century ship with destination to Rome to see the emperor. By God's providence, favor was placed in Paul's way. Verse 1 of the twenty-seventh chapter of Acts says, "They delivered Paul and some other prisoners to one named Julius, a centurion of the Augustan Regiment." The Bible points out this Roman officer will act kindly toward Paul. As the voyage got underway, the situation began to deteriorate. In the first century, navigation was depended on the sun, stars, and the wind to get to where they were going. Acts 27:22 paints a difficult situation for the apostle Paul and the other prisoners with him. "When neither sun nor stars appeared for many days and the storm continued raging, we finally gave up all hope of being saved." They were driven off course and now drifting in the sea. But the Lord assured Paul through the messenger of an angel that no life will be lost; however, they must run the ship aground on some island (Acts 27:22–26).

The source of deliverance for the apostle Paul was from the most unusual and unexpected source but deliverance did come. The sailors spotted land and began to prepare to move their way to the shoreline, but right before they got there, everything fell apart. "But the ship struck a sandbar and ran aground. The bow stuck fast and would not move, and the stern was broken to pieces by the pounding of the surf" (Acts 27:41 NIV). In the midst of this situation, the ship that they were planning on running aground to save their lives according Paul's assurance from the angel is now being broken to pieces. This is much like our natural life when the bottom has fallen out of our lives. What you thought was going to be there for you is now gone. What was once we thought was solid and secure is being broken into pieces. When we depend upon God for deliverance, it may not come through as we expect. We need to trust God for the outcome.

In the apostle Paul's situation, the circumstance got worse for him and other prisoners. The Roman soldiers on the ship plan was to kill the prisoners so that no one would escape, but here is the unlikely and unexpected source of deliverance. The Roman officer who was assigned to Paul kept the soldiers from carrying out their deadly intentions. The Roman officer commanded that those who could swim should jump overboard first and get to land. The rest were to get on planks or on other pieces of the ship. In this way, everyone reached land safely (Acts 27:44). It is amazing that God used the most unlikely source of deliverance in this disastrous episode to make life saving decisions to save the lives of the prisoners. For the people who could not swim, this was not a pretty picture. They were most likely using uncoordinated means to move or moving any way they could to get to the shoreline. The point is, they were moving toward the shoreline to safety. The Bible does not say whether the apostle Paul could swim or needed help, to get on one of those broken pieces to get to shore. In many ways, this is what our faith is like when we struggle. We are broken up and fearful of falling through the water and drowning, but God, through His grace, gives us what we need to go through. Our faith may feel minimal, but be willing to move toward God and not reject Him. Faith is not about your feelings; remember, it has a strong element of trust. Do not give into the temptation to move away from God in the middle of the struggle and brokenness. You cannot wait until you get it all together to move toward the shoreline, but as in this situation with the apostle Paul, you are literally riding on broken pieces but know that Jesus is always with you and He got your back in brokenness. God will use what you have; even if it is mustard seed faith, He will use it. Because you are trusting Jesus in your brokenness, someone else is coming in as well. All these people who heard the apostle Paul say, "They were all going to make it safely" were observing him.

We are not an island to ourselves. Your faithfulness to God even when it is minimal will make a difference in the life of others. There are also times when brokenness may hurt so bad that we do not know to pray. This is when our community plays a critical part in this journey. A community of people to be with you, pray for you and care for you. The community can be family, close friends, and the church. Just as the apostle Paul and those prisoners were not islands to themselves in their struggle, neither are we.

We must also be willing to seek professional counseling when needed. There is a social stigma in our culture and even within our Christian community on mental health. This stigma is the idea that those who seek help are stained, damaged, and weak-minded. According to MentalHealth.gov, mental health includes our emotional, psychological, and social well-being. It affects how we think, feel, and act. It also helps determine how we handle stress, relate to others, and make choices. Just as our physical bodies are subject to the fallen condition of this world, our mental health is also subject to life's stresses and trauma. We may need professional counseling along with spiritual help to bring balance in our mental well-being.

Serving While You Are Broken

It may seem unfair that even as you are going through, those of us who are ministry leaders or as a leader in your family may find yourself needing to help others while struggling in your own brokenness. During the time that I was serving as a deacon in my local church, I received phone calls from family members early one Sunday morning as I was preparing for the worship service. The calls were in sequence, one after the other, and the family members were not aware of each other's calls. Both family members were struggling over Jay's loss. Currently, it was about six months. Compounded on this situation was the loss of my baby sister to breast cancer just six months prior to Jay's death. There is no set time on how long people grieve because remember we are all different.

I spent some time consoling and encouraging the family members and doing my best to let them know we all will be okay. My hope was to instill perseverance and hope even as we grieve. By the time I was done talking to them on two separate phone calls, I was feeling very drained both physically and mentally. At our church, the first activity is for the pastor to pray with the deacons, trustees, and praise team before the start of morning worship service. My desire as I entered the church house was to just hear someone pray and encourage my spirit. Interesting that the same community that I said earlier played a critical part in this journey, I felt now was lacking at this moment. I truly needed to hear somebody say a few words of encouragement to lift me up, but before I was able to get into the office for prayer, the pastor informed me that he needed to talk to the praise team and for me to go out and conduct the praise service instead of the praise team.

I felt myself going into utter despair, but out of impulse, I said, "Yes, sir," when everything within me wanted to say, "No, sir, I cannot do this." Even in the house of worship, I felt going into a dark place feeling very drained physically and mentally. As I proceeded out of the pastor's office, I could not fathom how I was going to minister to this congregation in my condition. In the few moments, I felt how unfair this was when I am hurting and mentally exhausted that I am called to minister to people. I also felt betrayed by God for He knew my condition. He could have just allowed me to hear somebody say, "In the name of Jesus" or "It's going to be all right." Just a few words of comfort were all I was hoping for. I desired to just go out the emergency exit door, get in my car, and go home. That was my thinking, but God had another plan for me.

There was no other option but to somehow serve. In the few moments walking from the pastor's office door and into the main sanctuary, there was another desperate short prayer, "Lord, help me!" I asked another fellow deacon by the name of Doni Cross to assist me who by God's providence was available and an exceptionally talented singer. He had no idea that I felt broken, desperate, and uncertain as to what we were going to do and how things were going to turn out. The minister of music started playing an old familiar hymn, and Deacon Cross and I began to sing together. I had no choice but to trust God in my moment of desperation. In the process of singing the old hymnal, God renewed my spirit. He moved me from being uncertain, desperate, physically and mentally exhausted to exhilaration. This was only through the work of His Spirit. I could not see my way but had to trust God was going to make a way and He did. Your point of desperation may be totally different, but when it feels like faith is on thin ice, your faith balls down to trust that He will carry you through. God carrying you through implies that you are trusting Him when you do not see a way. This is when we must acknowledge to God that we are depending on Him, and we yield ourselves to His will. The feeling was unnerving and uncertain, but looking back at this moment, it gives me experience to know that I can have hope for the future because God is the object of my hope, He is in control and has proven Himself trustworthy. He will not let me fall and will not let you fall either.

A Biblical Picture of Faith on Thin Ice

The Bible speaks of many triumphs and victories over difficult circumstances. One of many characteristics of scripture is that it exposes the full person that include the victories and failures according to God's purpose for our learning and spiritual development. One of the most important and prominent biblical characters is Abraham. In the New Testament, the writer of Hebrews describes Abraham as a great man of faith: "By faith Abraham obeyed when he was called to go out to a place which he would receive as an inheritance. And he went out, not knowing where he was going" (Hebrews 11:8). The apostle Paul used the example of Abraham's faith as being accounted for righteousness before the Law of Moses was given. The great theological contribution is that faith is set in direct opposition to works in the matter of justification. Paul quotes directly from Genesis 15:6 in Romans 4:3: "Abraham believed God so God declared him to be righteous." Though Abraham was childless in his old age, God promised him, "All the families of the earth will be blessed through you" (Genesis 12:3). The great promise of God that appeared impossible provided a great test of faith, promise, and fulfillment for Abraham and his wife Sarah. Abraham's works were not credited as righteousness, but his faith was. Abraham, like other biblical figures of faith, died looking forward to the promise of the Messiah in the person of Jesus Christ. So with the significance of Abraham's faith, the Bible also describes some setbacks in his journey. This is just as there were setbacks in other biblical characters such as King David, Samson, and the disciple Peter in the New Testament. I believe that we learn from setbacks and as we look at scripture, God still made provisions despite those setbacks.

The two experiences to observe are first in Genesis 12:10–20 and second in Genesis 20:1–18. Genesis chapter 12 is early in Abraham's journey. At that time, he was known as Abram and his wife as Sarai. It was not until Genesis chapter 17 that God told him his name will no longer be Abram. Instead, he will be called Abraham for he will be the father of many nations. Likewise, God told Abraham that Sarai will no longer be Sarai. From now on, her name will be Sarah. For God promised to bless her and give Abraham a son from her. She will become the mother of many nations. Kings of nations will be among her descendants.

Early in Abram's journey, there was a famine in the land, and Abram went down to Egypt to dwell there for the famine was severe.

Sarai, his wife, was exceptionally beautiful, and Abram was concerned that the Egyptians will kill him and take Sarai to be Pharaoh's wife. When he got close to Egypt, Abram told Sarai to say that she was his sister. This is so they would spare his life and treat him well because of their interest in her. Just as he expected, the princes of Pharaoh saw her and commended her to Pharaoh's house with the impression that she was Abram's sister. This is a custom for incorporating unmarried women under the king's haram.[15]

As for Abram, he was treated well by the Egyptians under the premise that Sarai was his sister. But God intervened because clearly this was not God's divine plan according to what He promised in the beginning of Chapter 12. "I will bless those who bless you, and I will curse him who curses you. And in you all the families of the earth shall be blessed" (Genesis 12:3). God plagued Pharaoh and his house with great plagues. So Pharaoh summoned Abram and accused him sharply. He said, "What is this you have done to me? Why did you not tell me that she was your wife? Why did you say, she is my sister?" (Genesis 12:18–19). From the nature of the questions, Pharaoh was most likely enraged and humiliated. He would have taken Sarai to be his wife. Pharaoh commanded his men to escort Abram away with his wife and all their belongings. The sharp rebuke and humiliation were most deserving to Abram for lying. This scripture does not say how it was revealed to Pharaoh other than the great plagues that Sarai was married. The word *plagues* imply wound or disease. Perhaps when Pharaoh came close to making his move on this married woman, God made it clear to him that she is not his.

In the next experience in Abram's life, there are continuities with this same struggle in Egypt. Abram's journey continues in Genesis 20:1–18 who is now older and renamed Abraham and his wife Sarai renamed Sarah. The Lord appeared to Abraham in Genesis 17:1–7 to confirm His covenant with him—covenant meaning alliance, pledge between God and man. The promise of God to Abraham that He has made him a father of many nations. "I will make you exceedingly

---

[15] Geoffrey W. Bromiley, ed., *The International Standard Bible Encyclopedia*, Volume One: A (Wm. B. Eerdmans Publishing Co., 1979), 16.

fruitful and I will make nations of you, and kings shall come from you" (Genesis 17:6). As for Abraham's part and his descendants, they are to walk before God and be blameless. They are to set themselves apart by means of circumcision. The physical act of circumcision served as a sign of God's covenant relationship with His people that which was practiced by the Jewish nation for centuries. The emphasis in the New Testament is a changed heart. The sign of circumcision ultimately points toward the person of Jesus Christ and through Him a new life that is a new creation. For many, the act of circumcision became a practice of religious legalism, but the apostle Paul summarized it best: "In Him you were also circumcised with the circumcision made without hands, by putting off the body of sins of the flesh, by the circumcision of Christ" (Colossians 1:11). The significant events in Abraham's life speaks to his closeness to God in his journey. One of the most interesting events is when the Lord and two angels appeared to Abraham as men in Genesis 18:1. The Lord in this verse is translated "Jehovah"—self-existent or eternal. In this eighteenth chapter is a very personal interaction where the Lord reaffirms to Abraham that Sarah will have a son in their old age. Abraham intercedes for Sodom in verses 16 through 33 after the Lord made known to him of His intent to destroy the cities of Sodom and Gomorrah. So considering Abraham's close relationship with the Lord and now older, his judgment in Genesis 20:1–18 is worth examining.

Abraham migrated to the southern border of Canaan and settled in Gerar, a rich and well-watered pasture. While living in this new area as a foreigner, Abraham introduced his wife, Sarah, by saying, "She is my sister." This is the same deception he did in Egypt for fear of his life. So King Abimelech of Gerar sent for Sarah and had her brought to him at his palace to be one of his wives. From this culture's perspective, it was within the king's privilege to bring multiple wives into his palace.

Let me pause for a moment and explain that because the Bible describes the practice of polygamy by these kings; it does not teach polygamy. God's model for marriage is consistently one wife and one husband (Genesis 2:24–25; Mark 10:6–9; Matthew 19:4–6). This is a similar disastrous episode as in Egypt for Abraham and Sarah, but

God intervened on their behalf. God appeared to King Abimelech in a dream and revealed to him that he is surely a dead man because the woman that he has taken is already married. In King Abimelech's dream, he reasoned with God that he was innocent and not aware of her marital status. He reasoned with God further: "Lord, will you slay a righteous nation also? Did he not say to me, she is my sister? And She, even she herself said he is my brother" (Genesis 20:4–5). In his dream, God acknowledged Abimelech's position, and He was already aware of what was happening and did not allow him to come near Sarah. In God's provision, He withheld Abimelech from sinning against Him by not allowing him to touch Sarah. God instructed him to restore Sarah to Abraham as his wife and informed him that Abraham will pray for him and he shall live. God warned Abimelech if he did not follow his instructions, he shall surely die, and not just him as the king, but all his people.

Abimelech rose early from this nightmare, and he told all his servants about his incredibly detailed dream, and they were terrified. Abimelech summoned Abraham and said to him, "What have you done to us? How have I offended you, that you have brought on me and on my kingdom a great sin? You have done deeds to me that ought not be done" (Genesis 20:9). A rightful rebuke to Abraham for his deception. In Abimelech's attempt to understand Abraham's reason, he asked, "What did you have in view, that you have done this thing?" In other words, "What would make you to do such a thing?" Even with the humiliating rebuke by a king not known for serving the true God Jehovah, he tries to understand Abraham's reasoning for this deception.

Abraham's response in verses 11 to 13 is rather remarkable. Abraham acknowledged to the king that he thought his nation were not followers of God, and they will kill him on account of his wife. And he said Sarah is truly his sister because she is the daughter of his father, but not the daughter of his mother; she became his wife. Abraham said when God commanded him to leave his father's house he told Sarah, "This is your kindness that you should do for me: in every place, wherever we go, say of me, 'he is my brother'" (Genesis 20:13). Abraham's defense satisfied the king that there was not a direct and absolute falsehood, but he had told a moral untruth because there was intention to deceive. He lied! Abraham was not under pressure to save his life. This was a premeditated intent to deceive and the second offense of this kind. It exhibited distrust in God and His promise. The risk was Sarah being violated, the loss of integrity of his marriage, and if Abraham settled in this country and this dreadful situation, he would be tempted to forget about the promise. This was sin on Abraham's part.

I am not able to determine why Abraham was not able to trust God to protect him and his wife after all that he had been through up to this point and his direct encounters with God. The driver of his actions was most likely based on fear. The father of the Jewish nation and the Christian faith had insecurities as many of us have insecurities. Abraham's insecurities placed him in thin-ice situations with grave consequences for him and Sarah. But in these "faith on thin ice" moments, God grants us grace even in our failures. We can see in Abraham's failures where his faith may have been on thin ice, but God never abandoned Abraham. God made provisions for the promises He made to Abraham in Genesis 12:1–3. Jesus promised us that "I am with you always, even to the end of the age." Although we may feel alone and do not always understand why difficult things are happening to us, we hold on to God promises even through our insecurities and fears. Sometimes our insecurities, self-doubt, and fears can lead to bad judgments and decisions if we are not careful. As we get older, it's easy to look back and torture ourselves on the what-if thoughts: What if I made a better decision in my marriage, as a parent, what if I made better career and business decisions and other situations of life? The what if thoughts can lead to many regrets and depression about your life. To focus on regrets is grieving over bad choices and decisions. When memories come in the form of regrets, which can be a sense of loss, disappointment, and dissatisfaction, you must decide to act. We cannot change the past or recreate history, but we can change our perspective on how we view our past. We cannot let issues of our past make us fearful for the future. This will stifle forward motion in our life journey. The nature of our Christian walk is always faith forward. As we reflect on our lives, learn from the experience, and move forward and not be tortured with regrets! Ask God for help and take these steps:

Learn. Learn from mistakes, bad judgments, and disappointments. Sometimes learning from experience can mean we realize that we were moved more by fear, human self-centeredness and not trusting God as Abraham did in our review. Do not let fear cost future opportunities.

Be thankful. Be always thankful to God for by His grace and mercy He has brought you through the situations and you are still here. Always remember what He has done. The psalmist says, "Praise Him for His mighty acts; Praise Him according to His excellent greatness!"

Move forward. Be determined to allow how God has shaped you in the experience to move forward according to His guidance and purpose. Move forward knowing God's purpose for your life. If knowing and understanding God's purpose for your life is a big question mark, then it is time to make a life investment that will stay with you forever. Living according to God's purpose helps set your way forward by influencing life decisions, perspective, career paths, and other major life events. Start by seeking God to show you His purpose for your life. God has created each of us for His purpose and until we grasp this, there will always be a void. "For we are God's masterpiece. He has created us anew in Christ Jesus, so we can do the good things he planned for us long ago" (Ephesians 2:10 NLT). I will discuss this more in chapter 6, "The Shaping of Purpose."

When moving forward appears to hit an impasse, be mindful where your inner strength comes from. David said, "My help comes from the Lord, Who made heaven and earth" (Psalm 121:2). Consider the words of the apostle Paul who perhaps at one point struggled with issues of his past because he persecuted the church as a Pharisee prior to his conversion:

> I don't mean to say that I have already achieved these things or that I have already reached perfection. But I press on to possess that perfection for which Christ Jesus first possessed me. No, dear brothers and sisters, I have not achieved it, but I focus on this one thing: Forgetting the past and looking forward to what lies ahead. (Philippians 3:12–13 NLT)

The apostle Paul was determined to press forward without being weighed down by his past and ultimately to receive the heavenly prize for which God, through Christ Jesus is calling all of us. You have the power to move forward from regrets that may have weighed you down to live in liberation through His Spirit. Ask God for divine help to liberate you from the guilt and bondage of the past and live in the freedom of the adopted relationship as sons and daughters of God. Moving forward will involve persevering in trials as David will illustrate in the next segment.

A Picture of Faith Persevering in Trails

Psalm 40 is another psalm of King David. In many of David's writings, you will see confession of sin, expression of doubts and fears, asking God for help in times of trouble, and authentic praise and worship. I have a personal preference for the writers of the psalms. You will not find clichés but a pouring out of their true feelings and passion toward God. In verses 1–8, David present his petitions to God while at the same time offering his thanksgiving. David's expression follows the pattern in Philippians 4:6 in that we with thanksgiving let our requests be known to God. When things are not going well, it feels like an oxymoron—a self-contradictory condition. Sometimes it feels like what God wants us to do in our natural sense makes no sense.

But in the Spirit, it is right. The Bible encourages us to live according to the Spirit, the things of the Spirit (Romans 8:5b). To live according to the Spirit is to be under the predominate influence of the Spirit, which results in life and peace. The benefit of following the pattern of Philippians 4:6 is that the peace of God in verse 7, which surpasses all understanding, will guard your hearts and minds through Christ Jesus. I mentioned this scripture in the introduction. To take this a little further, God guards your mind like a soldier standing guard at his post. The King James Version of the Bible uses the word *keep* in Philippians 4:7. The Greek word is *phroureo*, and it means to guard, protect by a military guard, either to prevent hostile invasion, or to keep the inhabitants of a besieged city from flight. The enemy of our souls who is Satan will try to use ways to besiege our minds to get us thinking toward hopelessness, but God has a way out for us. This is a wonderful way that the apostle Paul used to describe the peace of God to Christians who were troubled, stressed, and facing persecution. The remedy for worry and stress is to take it all to God in prayer and the result is His peace that is not generated by the human mind. It can only come from the power of the Holy Spirit. It will not feel natural to offer thanksgiving to God while praying when you are going through very difficult circumstances in life, but the act of faith to reach out to God and not on feelings will result in the peace of God. The peace of God also protects us from confusion and helps us to make sound decisions and judgments.

Psalm 40 is a picture of how David's faith perseveres in his trails. He first acknowledges that God is the focus of trust. Not in his position and prestige as king or his skill as a warrior, but God is the focus of his trust. This has continuity with what I presented in the previous chapter that God is the object of our hope as one of the factors that empowers enduring hope. In verse 1, David said, "I waited patiently for the Lord." While he waited, he trusted and anticipated future deliverance from the present distress.

As in the Old Testament, we also trust God and hope for the future. So much of our faith is based on trusting God and as I stated previously, our faith has a strong component of trust. David has personal history with God as he expressed God hearing him and answering his prayers, "And He inclined to me and heard my cry." Sometimes, the most difficult thing to do is to wait on God to answer our prayers. When you don't have personal history with Him in answered prayer, then you must rely on the evidence of His word that speaks to who He is. As I said previously, consider just a few of His attributes that are far and above human attributes and how scripture confirms His nature.

In chapter 1, I discussed that "God is trustworthy" as the third factor that empowers enduring hope. Those of us who have personal history with God still struggle sometimes waiting on God for resolution of difficult circumstances. But we cannot forget what He already has done for us! To take this a step further, the psalmist writes "Praise Him for His mighty acts; Praise Him according to His excellent greatness!" (Psalm 150:2). This is a call to praise God for what He has done. Other psalms echoes the call to praise God for what He has done (Psalm 107:8, 145:4). Why would this seemly awkward act be done when we are facing life's difficult circumstances and trails? Because God is enthroned in the praise of His people (Psalm 22:3). It is easy to praise God when things are going well, but here is the benefit. When we praise God, God comes and sits down in the midst of the praise; when God shows up, everything that is not like God must leave![16] God is the center of David's trust so he further highlights what God has done: "He also brought me up out of a horrible pit, Out of the miry clay, And set my feet upon a rock, And established my steps. He has put a new song in my mouth—Praise to our God; Many will see it and fear, And will trust in the Lord" (Psalm 40:2–3).

Miry refers to mud, and *clay* refers to sticky. This reminds us that there are things in life that are not easily ridden of, and we must wait on God. The pit is a metaphor of calamity (sickness or battle). It would be wonderful that when we pray, God immediately sends the calamity away. But while we are in distress, God must be the center focus, so Satan does not gain a stronghold to put us in doubt and a state of harmful fear. David sends praise to God while in distress.

---

[16] Rodney A. Teal, *Reflections on Praise & Worship from a Biblical Perspective* (Rodney A. Teal, 2005), 15, www.revrodneyteal.org.

"Many will see it and give reverence to God." As you experience stress and difficult circumstances in your life, many will see your witness of what the Lord has done and is doing in your life journey. This is not pretending that nothing is wrong, but it is living life that reflects the promises of God's enduring hope.

Secondly, David's faith perseveres in his trails by being specific about his request. The circumstances that David was facing were extremely difficult and stressful as the next two verses reflects:

> Do not withhold Your tender mercies from me, O Lord; Let Your lovingkindness and Your truth continually preserve me. For innumerable evils have surrounded me; My iniquities have overtaken me, so that I am not able to look up; They are more than the hairs of my head; Therefore, my heart fails me. (Psalm 40:11–12)

In these verses, David expresses sorrow to God and is a window into his suffering. He was not able to look up because of the intensity of his suffering, being overwhelmed by evils that surrounds him and his own sin. His heart fails him so there is no inner strength to draw from. The New Living Translation of the Bible says, "I have lost all courage." David is a skilled man of war, and it appears that his identity was stripped because of overwhelming circumstance that surrounds him. What do you do and where do you turn? When you are not able to look up because of heaviness, and being waited down—look to His word and look to His promises. David appeals to God for His mercy and His loving kindness. He recognizes that it is God's truth that preserves. The word *preserves* in this context means to guard from dangers. The truth of God guards the soul and holds us together. David's appeals to what is known from an intimate relationship with God and not from a shallow relationship. David acknowledged his desperate condition, and by the act of his will, he looks to God. We must also decide to choose to look to God's eternal word for guidance and preservation. The Bible says, "The entirety of Your word is truth, and every one of your righteous judgements endures forever" (Psalm 119:160). The sixty-six books of the Bible are God breathed, meaning that all scripture is given by inspiration of God.

"All Scripture is inspired by God and is useful to teach us what is true and to make us realize what is wrong in our lives. It corrects us when we are wrong and teaches us to do what is right" (2 Timothy 3:16 NLT).

When we look to His word as David did, the Holy Spirit ministers to our souls because the Word is alive and will reveal us to ourselves. When our focus is only internally within us, this can lead to further despair and depression. We can recall other scripture that David used in times of trouble and distress:

Perhaps David recalls Psalms 3:3: "But thou, O Lord, art a shield for me, my glory, and the lifter up of mine head."

Perhaps David recalls Psalms 32:7: "You are my hiding place. You shall preserve me from trouble. You shall surround me with songs of deliverance."

Perhaps David recalls Psalms 27:5: "For in the time of trouble He shall hide me in His pavilion. In the secret place of His tabernacle, He shall hide me; He shall set me high upon a rock."

When circumstances make us feel like we are on thin ice, we must put our trust and confidence in the eternal word. Admittedly, I am an emotional person and sometimes desire an emotional touch by the hand of God. There are moments when we are not going to feel His presence or sense Him speaking, but His eternal word speaks loudly. God is not limited by what we feel in time and space. My condition, my illness, my hard-pressed circumstance are not obstacles to God. In due season, He will reveal Himself to us for we are never alone in Jesus Christ. Even when our faith is on thin ice, when our faith fails, God remains faithful to us.

When God Answers Your Prayers

Christians are not immune to grieving loss, struggle, shock, anger, and disappointments. Here is the shock and struggle of loss coupled with the answer from God that is assuming there were prayers for deliverance and protection preceding the loss of the loved one. This is certainly not in every circumstance because death can come suddenly and unexpectantly. For every parent, it is reasonable to assume we pray and hope for the safety and well-being of our children. Here again are the questions: Why did this happen to me or us with all the prayers going on, and did our prayers do any good? Even if we do not want to admit we had these questions, for many of us and particularly me these questions have come to mind. We touched on suffering in the "God Is Sovereign" section in chapter 1, but I want to work through the process when God answers our prayers, and when the outcome is not what we hoped for. There is a stage in our grieving process that we may experience denial of what has occurred. In my experience, there was denial coupled with hurt and disappointment with God's answer that ultimately led me through a strengthening process.

I was preparing a care package to send to Jay, and while preparing to mail it, a postal employee recognized what I was doing and recommended that I commit to Psalm 91. I believe she may have been a military parent as well and perhaps a believer and familiar with Psalm 91, which speaks of God's protection. I was generally familiar with Psalm 91, but not in detail. I thanked her and was very appreciative of the insight and encouragement from scripture. I recognize that God's Word is not a lucky charm or something magical that we manipulate to get our hearts desire. God's Word does provide provision that we can have the desires of our hearts but should be viewed with a sense of humbled submission. The Bible says, "Delight yourself also in the Lord, and He shall give you the desires of your heart. Commit your way to the Lord, trust also in Him, and He shall bring it to pass" (Psalm 37:4–5).

There is a strong element of trusting God in this scripture with what we desire. Our delight is in those things that are right and lawful in God's sight. So again, it is right that we pray for the health and well-being for those that we care about. The apostle John said, "Beloved, I pray that you may prosper in all things and be in health, just as your soul prospers" (3 John 1:2). The theme of Psalm 91 is God's protection, and my prayer like the prayers of all the Goldstar families is for our service member to come home safely without harm. Since my knowledge of Psalm 91 was general, I thought it was a good idea to memorize and get more familiar with it, and I asked Jay to memorize it with me. This was our goal to memorize it together. On a few occasions, when he called me on the Defense Switched Network—an internal telephone/data network within the Department of Defense—I would taunt him to see if he had it memorized yet. He would tell me it is in his helmet. That was his way of putting it in his head. Fortunately, working for the Department of Defense at that time gave me occasional access to talk to him. One cannot take this psalm as absolute protection from every form of evil circumstance, but there is great benefit when the Lord is our refuge. He can provide comfort in the storms of life as we have proven that God is trustworthy. We must be aware that deliverance is the will of God and that even if harm should come, we can still be secure in God knowing that nothing separates us from His love. The hope is our protection in the God who sees time and space where we live and eternity all at the same time.

At this point, Jay is a sergeant with additional responsibilities. As a young supply sergeant, he had the responsibility of running supplies to remote sites in his unit's area of operation. I would tell him to be careful because of the frequent attacks on military convoys. Now is the time for you to put your trust in God. He would respond to me, "Don't worry about me, I am immortal." Early in November 2004, he was able to take leave during midtour to be with his young family stationed in Germany where he was based. They were able to tour Paris, France, during his leave time and had an early Thanksgiving. I recall conversations between Kiona and Linda on what goes in the meal. We were incredibly happy they were able to spend time together. He returned to Iraq around mid-November. At this point, we felt confident that he will finish this tour and come back home safely. In my spirit, I had confidence that at this point God was going to allow his physical protection from dangers of this war and trusting in the words expressed in Psalm 91. Although in the back of my mind, I knew ultimately it was God's will.

We had a previous phone call in the middle of the night from Kiona on an attack on his unit, but he was okay. On Sunday morning, November 20, 2004, at two o'clock, I answered the phone with some reservation. It was Kiona with a strain in her voice. She had the strength to tell me that Jay was killed when his convoy was attacked. There was only silence from me as I listened in disbelief. I motioned to try to tell Linda but could not bring the words to my mouth to tell her. Linda was aware that phone calls this time in the morning could be serious, and me being silent in shock just made it more tense. She grabbed the phone and Kiona told her separately. The shock and numbness of this news is incredibly difficult to describe. I do not remember how long we were on the phone with Kiona, but in some awkward way, we tried to comfort her who, at this time, was only twenty-one years old. The army had already notified her in person in Germany. Not knowing what else to do, we called our pastor at the time, Rev. Dr. Frederick S. Jones. He answered the phone immediately in that early hour and comforted us and prayed with us. Only under the spiritual anointing of a pastor over a congregation was he able to minister directly to our need. I remember him saying in a sermon one Sunday morning that his wife could not understand how he could be sound asleep and wake up immediately when the phone rings in the middle of the night. He said, "It is only by the power of the Holy Spirit." This also speaks powerfully to the need for community support in times of loss. At eight o'clock that Sunday morning, an army chaplain and a young army officer arrived to officially notify us that Jay was killed in combat.

So with this, God answered our prayers for Jay's protection while deployed to Iraq. It was clear that this was God's will. There were several things going through my mind. Were my prayers sincere? Did I do something wrong or missed the mark? Why didn't God come through for us? It felt now that God was not making sense to me. This was a very confusing and overwhelming time, and it was difficult to think and hold clear thoughts together. This was the reason I deliberately wrote the "Bases of Our Hope" in the beginning of this book as foundational to my core beliefs, but as a husband and father, this was the most dreaded and difficult moment of our lives. Although I could not see it at that time, this was the beginning of God's strengthening process. I knew enough to realize that even in my confusion there was nowhere else to go except to seek the God of my salvation. Although hope seem fleeting, God was the only one that could help me. He had to become the "Object of my hope."

Fast-forward a few years to Memorial Day 2006, ABC *News Nightline* did a segment featuring Section 60, Arlington National Cemetery. This is the section where most of the fallen military members are laid to rest from Afghanistan and Iraq. The host, Mr. Terry Moran, wanted to bring attention to the soldiers laid to rest in this sacred place and their families who love them. I was interviewed on how we now remember Jay on Memorial Day and how this experience has now changed us forever. After the interview portion with me, and after the cameras were turned off and the crew broke down the equipment that was in our home, Mr. Moran asked me an honest question.

I believe during the interview I spoke about my prayers of hope that Jay will return home safely. Terry Moran leaned forward and asked me, "Weren't you disappointed when he didn't return home?"

The words that I used to answer his honest question were disingenuous. If I could go back in time to reflect on this question, I would have told him that I was devastated, and yes, I was disappointed that the answer to my prayers was different from what we expected. Perhaps relating that I am still growing and trusting God in our loss. I tried to present an image of strength in the middle of this devasting loss, but it was not a good witness. We present strength by showing how we depend on God when we struggle. The fact is, and I am saying it again, Christians are not immune to struggle from our losses and the difficulty that follows. Yes, we strive to be strong and leaning on our God for His strength, but pretending that nothing shakes us is not healthy and presents an incomplete picture of life. I was shaken, shocked, and numbed by the news of our loss along with great disappointment is what I should have told Mr. Terry Moran. I know I must look to Him, the God of my salvation. He is with us amid this horrible experience. He is the object of my hope, and by His sovereign will His answer to our prayers has come. So now what?

Like me and many others, we have a choice to make when faced with such loss. The human state of mind and emotional trauma of great disappointment is very real and cannot be denied. For some, this state of mind is exceedingly difficult to get beyond and move forward. Dr. James Dobson's book, *When God Doesn't Make Sense*, describes this state of mind in his forward of his book as the "betrayal barrier."

The idea of the "betrayal barrier" is this. It begins with extreme disappointment after we have relied on God to look after us. I reckon that most Christians, sooner or later, feel that God betrays them or uncaringly lets them down in some way. When I say they feel this, I refer to their perception of what appears to be going on. In truth, God never—ever—betrays us; He only appears to do so. But the feeling we have at a time like that is very strong. If we aren't careful,

we may say things to God—or about Him—that
we later regret.[17]

When our faith is tested, we must confront the question. Do I lean to my own understanding and face the risk of absolute despair and no hope? Or do I trust God? This answer is clear in wisdom literature of the Bible. "Trust in the Lord with all your heart and lean not on your own understanding; in all your ways acknowledge Him, and He shall direct your paths" (Proverbs 3:5–6). I know that some of us would hold to look to our inner strength and pull yourself up. The challenge is when there is no strength within to draw from, we put ourselves at risk of the enemy's deceptions and lies. In the Old Testament, David and his men faced a very painful situation when their base camp at Ziklag was attacked by the Amalekites and burned with fire and their families taken captive while they were away. The situation was so severe that they lifted their voices and wept until they had no more power to weep. The distress got to the point that his men spoke of stoning David because of their grief. The Bible says, "But David strengthened himself in the Lord his God" (1 Samuel 30:6). David strengthened himself, but the source of his strength was the Lord his God and not within himself. Because David strengthened himself in the Lord God and inquired what to do, the Lord God gave direction to pursue the enemy and recover all that was lost. In David's life journey, he consistently looked beyond himself for strength.

> From the end of the earth I will cry to you,
> When my heart is overwhelmed; Lead me to the
> rock that is higher than I. (Psalm 61:2)

> I cried unto the Lord with my voice, and he
> heard me out of his holy hill. I lay down and slept;
> I awoke, for the Lord sustained me. (Psalm 3:4–5)

---

[17] James C. Dobson, *When God Doesn't Make Sense* (Tyndale House Publishers, Inc., 1993), Kindle 8–9.

Leaning to my own understanding at this time would be leaning to uncertainty, confusion, and despair. Our faith has a strong element of trust as I stated before. It means to step out and trust him moment by moment and day by day to get beyond the betrayal barrier even if it feels risky and like you are on thin ice. Dr. James Dobson presents his perspective on faith and trust and how our trust takes the relationship a step further:

> It is not difficult for some of us to believe that God is capable of performing mighty deeds. After all, He created the entire universe from nothingness. He has the power to do anything He chooses. Having faith in Him can be a fairly straightforward thing. To demonstrate trust, however, takes the relationship a step farther. It involves the element of risk. It requires us to depend on Him to keep his promises, even when proof is not provided. It is continuing to believe when the evidence points in the opposite direction.[18]

We step out on faith by trusting God at His word, which relates directly to depending on Him to keep His promises. This is particularly important when our feelings and emotions point in the opposite direction of faith when we do not see the evidence of what we are hoping for. Our emotions can take us high and bring us down to dreadful low points. Trusting God at His word can bring stability when there is instability even within our own minds. It is here where God protects us from absolute hopelessness that makes us vulnerable to Satan's attacks. Trusting God is not going to always follow human logic. In my mind, it was reasonable to think that Jay would come home after some close calls and hardships midway on his tour. It was not reasonable to me that we would lose him shortly after returning to the war zone. Despite what I felt, my trust is taking Him at His

---

[18] Ibid., 109.

word. The words in Psalm 91 that Jay and I were memorizing takes on new meaning. God's Word must also be taken from the perspective of eternity and not only where we live in time and space. So I look to this same word that Jay and I were memorizing, and in this experience, God used as part of the strengthening process for me.

Psalm 91 is a beautiful picture of promise and protection. Verses 1 and 2 begins with two voices. Verse 1 is the voice of God: "He who dwells in the secret place of the Most High shall abide under the shadow of the Almighty." The word *dwells* mean to remain, so denoting a sustained nearness to God. This is our choice to make the effort in faith to stay near to Him. The secret places mean hiding place or covering and is in the physical and figurative sense. This is where I learn to remain close to God in my physical secret place and in my spirit where we can take refuge in God regardless to where we are. The benefit of dwelling in the secret place allows us to abide under His protection, which gives us confidence of His care and trust. The voice in verse 2 is our declaration of faith to trust in God: "I will say of the Lord, He is my refuge and my fortress; My God, in Him I will trust." The declaration of faith reflects a commitment to make God Jehovah both my refuge and fortress. This is my safe place and my stronghold; and it is in Him that I will find an unchanging, safe, and secure place to abide. In this declaration of faith is our trust in His protection and oversight of life. God protects us from fears that Satan will use to terrorize the mind. From my own personal experience, I present my fears to Him and total cares because of the refuge He promised me and has proven faithful as He has sustained me through many difficult internal struggles.

I am also encouraged to know that God was also Jay's refuge in the war zone. This was more than memorizing Psalm 91, but living it. On April 3, 2005, I received a rather detailed email from Jay's former company commander, Army Captain Jimmy Anderson. He presented a picture of Jay as one who was clearly inspirational and who led by example. No doubt that as a father and an army veteran, I appreciated him making it known to me the values Jay demonstrated as a young supply sergeant. But what has touched me the most was Jay's perspective about God and his demonstrated faith during the deployment. The unit conducted their own gospel service that Jay was a part of. Here is a portion of Captain Anderson's words:

> Sergeant Bryant kept a positive attitude and a healthy sense of humor throughout the deployment. Mr. Bryant his attitude and humor was absolutely contagious among the soldiers within and outside the unit. Everyone in the unit learned and greatly benefited from something invaluable from him, including myself. We learned through his mentorship, teachings, and actions that God's love transcends all barriers, whether they are racial or denominational. During our unit gospel service at the forward operating base, Jack Jr. was an integral part during the gospel service and consistently assisted with the awesome ministry team lead by Staff Sergeant (Minister) Sorrel and Specialist (Minister) Joseph. During the gospel service we all witnessed saints accepting Jesus as Lord and being baptized into the family of believers, many re-directions, several acknowledging their call to ministry and others receiving their breakthrough. All I can say is "God is Good!"

I had to think for a moment that this was the same boy as a young teenager, getting him ready for church on Sunday mornings was a major endeavor. But at this point as a young man and by the witnesses of others, God was Jay's refuge in the war zone. It would have been my personal preference that his spiritual growth took place in a safer place, but the fact is it took place. I believe Jay dwelled in the secret place of the most high God while deployed. I believe that Jay trusted God to be his refuge and his fortress, and God used him to be a mentor and teacher of others. He was frequently on the road making supply runs but never in his writings and from the comments of others that he demonstrated fear with the risks that his unit faced every day. From the reality of where he was, there were certainly concerns in a war zone. But he did not operate under fear and conducted himself in such a way that demonstrated confidence and assurance of God's protection. The next four verses in Psalm 91 speak of this assurance.

> Surely He shall deliver you from the snare of the fowler And from the perilous pestilence.
> He shall cover you with His feathers, And under His wings you shall take refuge;
> His truth shall be your shield and buckler. You shall not be afraid of the terror by night,
> Nor of the arrow that flies by day, Nor of the pestilence that walks in darkness, Nor of the destruction that lays waste at noonday. (Psalm 91:3–6)

These verses continue to echo the theme of verse 1 with assurance of dwelling under His protection. Under His wings, there is refuge and covering. Picture the mighty wingspan of an eagle protecting its young. His eternal word shall be our shield and buckler. The shield or buckler was the oldest and most common weapon of defense in Israel's army. A large shield was used by the heavy-armed infantry that covered the whole body and a small light shield was used by archers and for hand-to-hand fighting.[19] His eternal truth protects us from error, lies, and deception from the enemy. The psalm speaks of freedom from fear of what terrorizes us in the physical and in the spiritual realm. This does not mean we are to be careless of known dangers nor does it eliminate situations that catches us off guard, but God lifts us from a condition of fearfulness. I define a condition of fearfulness where harmful fear is dominating our lives. Fearfulness works against our faith particularly when it comes to trusting God at His word when it feels risky.

---

[19] Charles F. Pfeiffer, Howard F. Vos, John Rea, eds., *Wycliffe Bible Dictionary* (Peabody: Hendrickson Publishers, Inc., 2005), 151.

The Bible says, "For God has not given us a spirit of fear, but of power and of love and of a sound mind" (2 Timothy 1:7). If God has not given us a spirit of harmful fear or a spirit of timidity than it is coming from Satan and his demons. The Bible also says, "For you did not receive the spirit of bondage again to fear, but you received the Spirit of adoption by whom we cry out, Abba, Father" (Romans 8:15). Our relationship with God the Father helps us to walk in this life with self-assurance and courage by the power of the Holy Spirit. He helps me to move forward without the dreadful fear of wondering how. I am trusting him at His word. The final three verses are of particular interest to me.

> Because he has set his love upon Me, therefore I will deliver him; I will set him on high, because he has known My name. He shall call upon Me, and I will answer him; I will be with him in trouble; I will deliver him and honor him. With long life I will satisfy him, And show him My salvation. (Psalm 91:14–16)

At this point it, would be my desire to look into Jay's soul and relate how this portion of scripture relates to him. God did not give me that insight, but it speaks directly to me. The Hebrew writer in the New Testament says, "For the word of God is living and powerful, and sharper than any two-edge sword, piercing even to the division of soul and spirit, and of joints and marrow, and is a discerner of thoughts and intents of the heart" (Hebrews 4:12).

The word of God through the Holy Spirit reveals to us who we are, and this word reminded me about God's hand of protection and deliverance in my own life. Early in my teenage years, I have directly experienced God's hand of protection and deliverance because I know His name. On a summer night in July 1971, a childhood friend wanted me to walk with him to his girlfriend's house. That was not a very exciting thing to do to for me, but at the moment, I was bored out of mind and desired to go somewhere or just anywhere. There was a rule in my mother's house for us younger siblings to not venture too far away from the city block of 2200 Franklin Street in North Philadelphia because of the dangers of gang warfare in the seventies. I violated this rule because I was so bored. It was quiet that night, and I felt confident we would be fine. We made it to his girlfriend's house, and I listened to a lot of teenage squabbles back and forth until he decided it was time to leave.

As we walked back, I was not paying attention to where we were going. I was just so happy go lucky to go somewhere and do something that evening. As we were walking, to my horror, out of the darkness of an open lot were about twenty-five young boys that surrounded me and my friend. The exact number escapes me, but it seems like an army to my sight. They questioned my friend about his affiliation. Being young and black, there was always the risk of being mistaken for being affiliated with a rival gang. That was my assumption for my childhood friend. They questioned him, and the conversation did not go well, and some of the gang members began striking him with clubs. I decided to run but was quickly overtaken, and they proceeded to beat me with sticks and clubs. I could not remember what they were using but felt the impact of multiple strikes on my head, face, and body. As I covered my head with my hands, there was one name that I knew to call on. I called on the name of Jesus. It was just Jesus. I was beaten to the ground, and when they stopped, somebody came back and punched me in the back or what I thought was a punch. The reality was one of the gang members decided to come back and stab me in the back. I heard one of them say, "That's enough," and they ran off. I thought I could get up and find my way back to Franklin Street, but not knowing I was stabbed, that may not have been possible.

Just as the unexpected horror came out of the darkness was an unexpected voice of a woman. I remember her saying, "Oh my god." She came over with a companion and picked up this fifteen-year-old boy and put me into her car. This was a divinely lead act because many adults were killed in gang violence just by being caught in the middle of it. This woman took a stand in a dreadful situation. She never identified herself. As far as I knew, she could have been an angel driving a Volkswagen Beetle because I remember the shape and the distinctive sound. I was able to tell her my address, and she took me home to Franklin Street. My oldest sister was outside in a car with a friend, and they observed the women bringing me to the door. My sister did not recognize it was me except for the clothes I was wearing that day. The women told my mother inside the house who I was and that I needed immediate medical attention. My oldest sister, her friend, and my mother rushed me to Temple University Hospital where I received the treatment that I needed. The stab wound resulted in a collapsed lung and hospitalization for a week, but by God's grace, He delivered me, and I recovered.

Psalm 91:14–16 is directly tied to my experience. I called upon Him, and He answered me. He was with me in trouble. I still faced a horrible environment of the shadow of death, but God protected by the promise and power of His word. As I reflect on His word, I cannot help but to be strengthened by what He did for me. God by His word delivered me and honored me to speak of what He is able to do. At the age of thirteen, I decided to give my life to Jesus Christ during a revival service at a onetime converted movie theater called the Metropolitan Theater on Broad and Poplar Street in north Philadelphia, now called the Met. My admiration is the historic significance since 1908 and the physical place where I met Jesus Christ when it was used as a church. So in reflection on this scripture, I believe because I have set my love upon Him, He delivered me, and I have reason to believe in God's protection. These last three verses speak of the spiritual connection and intimacy with Him and through the dangers, He has allowed me to live and see His grace. The physical dangers were real, but I walked with the assurance that He was with me and was with Jay. By this we are assured that we will never be alone. With the spiritual connection, even if the physical life is removed from us, we are immediately ushered into His presence.

I am truly grateful for God's grace and mercy demonstrated at this early stage of my life, but there was something that I had to do in light of this horrific event. Fast-forward to the age of twenty-four and now a college graduate, on active duty in the United States Army, and married with young children. From fifteen years old up to this time, I carried frustration and anger over what happened to me on that summer evening in July. I was angry because of the unfairness and the beating of an innocent child. Although never demonstrated anger outwardly, this was always internalized within me. A portion of innocence was lost within me because of the violence of this attack. I was also internally frustrated because of the helplessness it made me feel. I could not identify the attackers, so there were no arrests and no convictions or accountability. Within me, there was hatred for the individuals that assaulted me, and this was carried within me as a young man. As I quoted previously, the Word of God is "a discerner of the thoughts and intents of the heart." One day, I was alone in our home in North Carolina, and the Holy Spirit confronted me with a familiar scripture in my mind. This was so strong that I was compelled to consider the thoughts in my mind. God as big as He is will never force someone into action. As human beings, we have the volitional ability to choose our course of action. I could have resisted but decided to allow the Holy Spirit to guide me in this thought process. This scripture in the book of Mark speaks directly about our response to forgiveness: "And whenever you stand praying, if you have anything against anyone, forgive him, that your Father in heaven may also forgive you your trespasses" (Mark 11:25–26).

I remember the moment and the scripture for they were truly clear in my mind. What was not clear to me was how could God require me to forgive those people for what they had done to me. In my mind, they did not deserve my forgiveness, but only my hate for attacking an innocent kid. But His word was clear, and I could not get away from it; and considering our human condition, we truly do not deserve forgiveness either, but Jesus gave it to us who believe. The choice was to step out on faith and trust God with something that seems not possible or continue in my present state of mind. I felt that my faith was on thin ice and failing at this. I prayed one of the most awkward prayers of my life. I knew this was only by faith and not about what I was feeling at the moment. So I prayed; it was more like I mumbled the words "Lord, I forgive these young boys for assaulting me with the attempt to take my life." This prayer was an act of my will and trust that God was going to help me do this. Remember again that our faith has a strong element of trust. The feeling was not there, but my trust was that if God required me to do this, then He will give me the power to accomplish His will. I cannot tell you the moment or the time that He delivered me, but deliverance did come, and God lifted me from the hatred of these people, the frustration and helplessness that I felt for almost nine years.

Unforgiveness will only eat you up from the inside out. I felt that I was punishing them with my hatred, but in reality, the unforgiveness in my heart was punishing me. As I look back at this event from the perspective of healing through forgiveness, rather than the frustration, hatred, and helplessness, I see God's grace and mercy for me. I look back at the event as a testimony of deliverance, and it brings peace and assurance that God is ever with us. So what does this experience have to do with Jay and Psalm 91?

God reminded me that He sees the total picture of my life and that He proved that He is the same God who was with me, was with Jay. Being reminded of this was strengthening to me. When God answers our prayers, He answers them from His eternal perspective. He sees the whole process of your life to include the joyful and tearful events of life. As we studied Psalm 139, remember our days are fashioned for us by God, like a potter who forms a vessel according to His will and purpose. God allows the circumstance to shape and mold us. God's answer to our prayers was difficult to bear, but in this process, I was reminded that God is trustworthy even in hard circumstances that test our faith. We all must know through God's Word that "when your faith is tested, your endurance has a chance to grow" (James 1:3 NLT). God has allowed me to grow even in this grief burden that I thought was unbearable. He made it possible to bear because He gave me the assurance that He was with me. I write this with the assurance that God was Jay's refuge in the warzone just as He was my refuge in this whole strengthening process. To God be the glory! Our enduring hope is empowered by the three factors: God is the object of our hope, God is sovereign, and God is trustworthy.

When God Answers Your Prayers: The Impact on Marriage

When we prayed for Jay's return, it was a collective prayer. So when he did not return, it was a collective grave despair. There are many strains on marriages, and nothing can be more strenuous than the loss of a child. The previous section I focused primarily on me, but make no mistake; the loss of Jay sent shock waves to the marriage as well. This is not something that parents can imagine or would want to. One observation is that although we are husband and wife, we are still individuals and will work through grief differently. As an army veteran I can identify with Jay and swell in pride to think of him as a husband, father, and sergeant in the United States Army. When people would tell us that Sgt. Jack Bryant Jr. was a hero, it brought pride to me, but it was no comfort for Linda as a grieving mother.

For Linda, that is her little boy, and she is missing her son and her heart aches for her son. This does not minimize the grief of a father, but it is important to know there are differences. For a mother who gave birth to a child, this is a level of intimacy that men will not fully comprehend because of the natural bond between a mother and her child. When you realize there are differences, I believe you are better equipped to understand that there may be moments when we will not fully understand what is going on internally as individuals. Our response to grief as individuals will manifest in ways that are unexpected. The year 2004 was particularly challenging for our families. On April 19, 2004, I was informed by one of my siblings that our baby sister's condition for breast cancer had deteriorated to the point that there was nothing more that the doctors could do. On June 28, 2004, my youngest sister passed away from breast cancer, leaving a thirteen-year-old daughter and a sixteen-year-old son. Then six months later, we lost Jay on November 20, 2004. This was a double blow to our souls.

As I stated before, these situations can leave you numb, but in the longer term, it left me not motivated to do some of the things that are considered normal and routine. I was not motivated to fix things and make improvements to the new home we just moved into in April of that same year. For me, it was difficult even over a period of a few years to engage in home improvements or even engage in simple maintenance tasks. This was not evident to Linda and, frankly, not evident to me during this time. When it is not easy to understand each other, it is time to seek help through counseling. The counsel of a qualified third party can help when it is difficult to understand differences and to assist in sorting out and get to the root of issues. I encourage married couples to seek professional counseling when navigating the trauma and difficulties of losing a child. My biggest regret in this experience is that we did not seek professional counseling. But what I am grateful for is that there were some foundations we laid early on that helped us navigate through this storm.

As I reflect on our experience, the best approach is to be committed to loving unconditionally and to be committed to the relationship. Why is this so important? First love is not easy, and there are so many misconceptions as to what it is. Second, there will be moments when the relationship is not always pleasant, and we must be committed to working through problems. There may even be moments when we may not like each other but consider what is at the core of the relationship. At the core of the relationship is love. In the lyrics of Tina Turner's 1984 hit song "What Love Got To Do

With It" she defined love as a "*secondhand emotion*," but it is so much more. In fact, it is not all about emotion.

Years ago, Linda and I attended a "Becoming Soul Mates Seminar" facilitated by Drs. Les and Leslie Parrott, well-known authors, and practitioners in helping others build healthy relationships. One of the things we gathered from the seminar is that in the marriage relationship there is a love triangle. Imagine at the bottom of the triangle is commitment, and on each side is passion and intimacy. The passion and intimacy in the relationship may sway. There may be periods when intimacy and passion become difficult when the relationship is stressed such as with grieving loss and other situations. At the bottom of the triangle is commitment, and within commitment is the willful side of love. These are decisions that are not always based on how we feel at the moment but based on unconditional love and a lifelong commitment to a covenant relationship. The covenant relationship refers to a biblical model where marriage is a lifelong relationship committed before God. What we can learn from this concept is that commitment must be foundational for the marriage relationship to navigate through the difficult times. That is the willingness to work through the problems when it is not convenient, when it is awkward, and when it is even painful to do so. Here is the reality that we face. It takes the willingness of two people to work on commitment in a marriage relationship. God had given us the volitional ability to choose our path—to make a decision. We must choose to love. When this is troubled by one or both husband and wife, work must be done to get both or one to the point to work on the commitment to love preferably through counseling. Individuals will choose their own path, and we cannot force anyone to love us no matter what we do for them. God will not force us to love Him. Our love for Him is our own choice, or else, it will not be a true relationship.

So how should we define love in marriage? In our culture, the definitions are many and varied. I will never claim any expertise on marriage, but after over forty years of marriage, I can make some observations and see clearly how the teaching in scripture can help us. The safest definition to start with is to observe how scripture treats the marriage relationship. The most prominent word for *love* in the New Testament is translated *agapao*. When the apostle Paul commanded husbands to "love their wives," he used this word (Ephesians 5:25). The word means "affection for persons" "to love someone more than one's life."[20] This love is totally unselfish, which seeks not its own satisfaction, nor even affection answering, but that strives for the highest good of the one loved.[21]

There is another expression in the New Testament called *phileo*, which compares to *agapao* but is distinguished to more represent "tender affection."[22] Paul, however, did not use this word. The love in marriage is inclusive of unconditional love and commitment toward each other. It is also appropriate to have the friendship and affection along with the romantic love, emotional and sexual intimacy that God designed in marriage from the beginning. So what was the apostle Paul after when he gave this command in Ephesians 5:25? The kind of love that the apostle Paul is targeting is the love that Jesus Christ has for His church and gave Himself for it. This is the model for marriage.

For those of us who are mistake-makers and full of imperfection, this is a high order. I will be the first to raise my hand as a member in the mistake-makers club. Christian marriages are not perfect by any stretch of the imagination, but God has given us the model as the foundation, and I would hold, He has given us everything we need to do His will. Remember the love triangle that I described earlier. At the base of the triangle is commitment, and within this commitment is the willful side of love. The agapao love is what holds the other elements of the love triangle together. This is what helps hold a marriage together when health challenges come about and other difficult circumstances. The apostle Paul goes on to explain how

---

[20] Walter Bauer, *A Greek-English Lexicon of the New Testament and Other Early Christian Literature* (The University of Chicago Press, 1979), 4.

[21] Frances Foulkes, *Ephesians: An Introduction and Commentary, vol. 10, Tyndale New Testament Commentaries* (InterVarsity Press, 1989), 162–163.

[22] W. E. Vine, Merrill F. Unger, and William White, *Vine's Complete Expository Dictionary of Old and New Testament Words* (Thomas Nelson Publishers, 1996), 382.

this kind of love behaves. He used a similar word in 1 Corinthians 13:1–7. This passage reads like a hymn and is directed to the problems of the Corinthian Christian church. It is comprehensive in its description of how we are to treat each other but the application can be easily applied to marriage for both husband and wife. We all may want to take an inventory of ourselves and consider where we are in our love commitment. I don't believe God will give us a guidelines and instructions to abide by without empowering us to achieve what He desires. As the apostle Paul discusses how love behaves, we can be assured that there is power behind the word and the walk of faith requires us to trust Him at His word. "Your word is a lamp to my feet and a light to my path" (Psalm 119:105).

In the apostle Paul's letter to the Corinthian church, he addresses unconditional love in 1 Corinthians chapter 13. In Christian circles, this is often described as the love chapter. In the context of chapters 12 and 13, Paul is addressing the issues of the lack of love and concern for one another in the Corinthian church. The emphasis is the proper use of spiritual gifts, which all are treated equally and valued equally and a part of one unified body. Paul instructs at the end of chapter 12 that you should earnestly desire the most helpful spiritual gifts in the body of Christ, but now let me show you a more excellent way. In other words, let me now show you a way of life that is best of all. Paul goes into detail on how unconditional love is to behave in verse 4–7.

> Love suffers long and is kind; love does not envy; love does not parade itself, is not puffed up; does not behave rudely, does not seek its own, is not provoked, thinks no evil; does not rejoice in iniquity, but rejoices in the truth; bears all things, believes all things, hopes all things, endures all things. (1 Corinthians 13:4–7)

The idea of looking at these verses is to look at love that is at work. Love involves work and perseverance. The apostle Paul is addressing issues within the Corinthian church as they are attempting to use their God given spiritual gifts without showing love for one another, which makes their spiritual gifts useless and profit them nothing. I want to lift some nuggets of truth from these verses and apply them to the marriage relationship.

Love suffers long and is kind.

The apostle Paul opens with this statement. Even for Christians, the idea of suffering long is not an easy concept. The word *suffers* refers to patience—patiently endure. In marriage, patience is a virtue that will help the relationship in many ways. Many of us bring strengths and weaknesses to the relationship. One may be more patient with young children than the other, or like me, learning how to handle household finances early in the relationship. This was not a strength I brought into the relationship, but thank God, not too many disasters. This took a lot of patience on Linda's part. Patience is necessary to work through many challenges together, particularly when we don't have immediate solutions to problems. Kindness can take the form of looking out for each other's needs. As we get older with health challenges, kindness becomes important when one needs assistance to function and live life fully.

"Love does not parade itself, is not puffed."

A boastful and prideful perspective may be harmful to the relationship. If we are too prideful to admit when we are wrong in the relationship, this could lead to more frustration and resentment with your spouse. A boastful perspective will hinder the need for change when it is necessary to work on the relationship. Built-up frustrations can lead to blow ups in inappropriate ways.

"Love does not behave rudely, does not seek its own."

To behave rudely is to act unbecoming or acting inappropriately. If we say we love someone, acting rudely is not loving and is not relationship building but more tearing it down when the behavior is consistent. We all have life objectives and goals, but sometimes, it may be necessary that major decisions in the household are to consider the well-being of your spouse and your family. This may mean a change in jobs or even relocation. The decisions are not always exclusively about you. The seventh verse in this portion of scripture describes essentials for moving forward.

"Bears all things, believes all things, hopes all things, endure all things."

What this last verse says for marriage is to strive and fight to save your marriage despite the difficulty and disappointment. Continue to trust God despite suffering and loss. In our human strength, this is impossible, but by the power of the Holy Spirt, nothing is impossible for Him.

"Love never fails."

As the apostle begins his concluding thoughts on this subject, he takes the scripture a step further. The first three words of verse 8 says, *"Love never fails!"* Make no doubt, we do fail! We cannot claim that our love never fails. But because love is the very essence of God Himself for *"God Is Love"* (1 John 4:8,16), therefore *"Love never fails."* We can look toward the love of God who loved us so much that Jesus came and died for our sins and rose again. The reason love never fails is because it points toward a person, and that person is Jesus Christ.

The Lord God is our enduring hope for marriages. This is who we look to for help with the biblical model of love. For us chief mistake-makers, those of us who continue to struggle sometimes in our marriages, how do we navigate the challenges that we face? The privilege that we have is we can ask for help. I often pray to God to show me how to love my wife and, in my daily devotion, show me where I am falling short. He will do that for you as he has done for me. But this request cannot be done in arrogance, rudeness, and self-centeredness but with humble submission unto God. This is the God who knows about our human condition and acquainted with all our ways. In one of my divinity classes, the professor broke us up into small groups and gave each group a preselected scripture. The assignment was to pray, study, and meditate on the scripture and come back to the group and give a reflection of what the scripture revealed to us. The scripture given to my group was Luke 7:11–15, but I included verses 16 and 17 to provide more context to the story.

> Now it happened, the day after, that He went into a city called Nain; and many of His disciples went with Him, and a large crowd. And when He came near the gate of the city, behold,

a dead man was being carried out, the only son of his mother; and she was a widow. And a large crowd from the city was with her. When the Lord saw her, He had compassion on her and said to her, "Do not weep." Then He came and touched the open coffin, and those who carried him stood still. And He said, "Young man, I say to you, arise." So he who was dead sat up and began to speak. And He presented him to his mother. Then fear came upon all, and they glorified God, saying, "A great prophet has risen up among us"; and, "God has visited His people." And this report about Him went throughout all Judea and all the surrounding region.

The key verse that has changed my outlook was the thirteenth verse where Jesus had compassion on the widow. Compassion is closely tied to mercy and relates to God's love as a move to help the miserable. A widow in biblical times with no family support other than the only son means a life of poverty. Jesus first had compassion for her as a grieving mother. His words to the widow when He saw her were "Do not weep." By His word, He spoke life to the young man who was dead and by Jesus's word sat up and began to speak. Second, Jesus had compassion on her for the impoverished condition that she would have faced as a widow in that time. Jesus's reaction to the widow's condition of the loss of her only son revealed to me that I lacked compassion for Linda as a grieving mother in the loss of our son. Although I may not comprehend all the things that she was dealing with internally, the experience changed my focus from a desire to quickly move forward in our grieving to striving to better understand her in the life journey that we are both on. I don't believe there is a set timetable for grieving. The experts may put us at various stages, but the bottom line is we are all different and will grieve differently and must make the effort to understand each other's needs. I am a firm believer that God will meet you where you are and provide for your needs.

One last thought on the impact on marriage. We must not engage in finger-pointing or blame for the death of a child or loved one. It is very easy to look back and wish that we could have done this or done that. There is always room for improvement on better parenting. Every parent will fit in that category. It was my decision to encourage Jay to consider the military as an option after high school, but this will not be a source of guilt for me or for Linda. Although we are still striving on this journey, we are striving together years later. Our enduring hope is empowered by the three factors: God is the object of our hope, God is sovereign, and God is trustworthy.

The Battles Within

I wondered how to handle this chapter and where to place it. When I started this journey, the intent was to simply witness how God is a keeper in a time of grief and trouble and our experience with the living God with our loss. I was amazed how He demonstrated Himself to us in this journey and gave us hope that I can only say twenty years later is enduring. But I encountered two veterans who have influenced my journey in documenting our experience. This made me more determined to present a message of hope that is not only enduring in this life but also for all eternity. I said in the introduction that for many of our veterans there is a battlefield within that they face because of the effects of their combat experience. There are veterans who bear the scars—some seen and unseen. We must never forget! So my goal was expanded to not just document our journey with the God of our hope but to make every effort to prove that our hope is enduring and empowered by the three factors: God is the object of our hope, God is sovereign, and God is trustworthy.

My hope in writing is to also help our veterans and others be lifted out of hopelessness and experience enduring hope. The first veteran I met will only identify as Robert to protect his privacy. There was only one encounter, but it was enough to make an impact on me. I met Robert when he came to my house to repair my old school fifty-six-inch tub TV. These were the TVs that weighed a ton, but it was still functional. My old-school TV got zapped by an electrical surge, and I was determined to make it alive again. I called Robert's company with the hope of saving the last large tub TV I owned. Robert arrived at my house, a well-dressed and very professional young man. I described to him what I thought was the problem of the unit not working, and he began to disassemble it to troubleshoot. As he was working and moving the TV away out of the display cabinet, he noticed pictures of Jay on the wall to the left of him, along with a glass shadow box containing his medals and folded flag. I explained who Jay was and the circumstances of his death. Robert then started sobbing uncontrollably. I am sure this was not what he intended to let happen, but when he was able to regain his composure, he told me that he was an army linguist and deployed to Iraq and Afghanistan on extended tours. Being an army linguist, he was serving in a critical military occupational skill (MOS) and unfortunately required extended tours in these war zones because of the critical need for his skills.

Robert shared with me a pivotal point in his life. During his deployment in Iraq, he was seriously wounded during an attack by insurgents. When one of his army friends was assisting him during the attack, he was killed. Robert was devastated over what happened; as I recalled, he told me he would rather go back to the war zone and take his rest. This is an indication that he was not valuing his own life. I told him that this was not his fault that his friend was killed in the process of helping him. I wanted to encourage him that God is able to keep you during times of trouble, but Robert quickly pointed out that he rejects God and do not want to hear anything of that nature. His only comfort he had was alcohol. In an effort to connect, I told him that we share a common bond in that we both lost someone that we cared for deeply, and he is not alone in what he was feeling. I gave Robert my card in a hope of staying connected. He finished his work at my home and departed with a circuit board that was defective from the TV.

It was very difficult for me to hear Robert's personal experience. I knew some veterans were struggling with their combat experience, but this was an encounter that has touched me deeply. In about two weeks, Robert returned to my home and replaced the defective part of the TV. I observed that he wanted to avoid any discussion from the previous visit. He kept a professional composure and completed the work that he came to do. I also observed perhaps some embarrassment in his unintentional reaction to Jay's story, and I am sure he wanted to be careful not to lose control. As Robert was leaving my house, I observed a young man that experienced deep trauma on the battlefield with the loss of a friend attempting to help him. Also, the result of overwhelming guilt that he carries with his loss. When Robert left for this second time, it was my hope that he would contact me to help him. For I am sure that he is not alone with the battles within. The TV played for a very short time, but eventually, the lines on the picture appeared and the problem was clearly not fixed. It was also very clear to me that the old-school TV that I wanted to save was not the real purpose of this encounter. God allowed this encounter with this young veteran to show me what hopelessness can do to a person and prayerfully share a seed of hope that would take root in his life.

What do we do with the battles within? This is what I intend to address in this chapter, but first I must also discuss another encounter with a young veteran. I can only believe this is by God's providence as I strive to understand the battles that veterans continue to face. Linda and I met another veteran struggling with overwhelming guilt, but very a different circumstance. The second veteran I will only identify as Erick to protect his privacy. Linda and I try to make a trip to Arlington National Cemetery on Veterans Day and Memorial Day to honor Jay and other veterans. On one Memorial Day, we traveled alone. Typically, we will have a few of the grandchildren along with one of our daughters but not on this trip. Erick walked up to us where we were sitting at Jay's grave site and introduced himself. He told us that he was in the same unit with Jay, and on that day of Jay's last convoy, he was scheduled to go but was afraid. Jay decided to take the convoy and, in my mind, only after he made a few colorful words.

Erick started sobbing because of the guilt that he felt for not going on the convoy as scheduled. We felt the pain that he was feeling, and our desire and response was to comfort him and not agonize over what happened. We wanted to let him know that there was no anger and resentment from us but for him to live in the liberty of the Spirit of God. I believe the Holy Spirit guided us to have compassion rather than anger for what Erick just told us. For in relationship with Jesus Christ, He promised us another Helper—this is the Holy Spirit. Jesus said, "The Spirit of Truth, whom the world cannot receive because it neither sees Him nor knows Him; but you know Him, for He dwells with you and will be in you" (John 14:17). The Holy Spirit enables us to have peace even when faced with inward difficulties and heaviness of heart. This is the hope that we have for Erick. I exchanged phone numbers with the intent to keep in contact. To be honest, when you are presented with information like this, being human, your mind will wonder. You wonder what if the situation was different. What if Erick was on the convoy instead of Jay? I believe we were led by the Holy Spirit to comfort Erick and not condemn or criticize him. But at the same time, realize how this type of information can affect you. It made us think about the situation and the moment Jay's convoy was attacked.

On that day, when we got home from Arlington National Cemetery, my oldest daughter Denie told me she observed me in the kitchen with a coffee mug in my hand, standing and staring at the mug as if frozen. When she got my attention, I was only able to tell her at the moment, "Your mom is upstairs." Sometimes, these moments leave you without words. I heard a speaker describe Psalm 91:1 as the 911 for our help. "He that dwelleth in the secret place of the Most High shall abide under the shadow of the Almighty." I most certainly believe this! I described Psalm 91 in chapter 3. As I said previously, the word *dwells* in this psalm means to remain so denoting a sustained nearness to God. Again, this is our choice to make the effort in faith to stay near to Him. The second verse in Psalm 91 is our declaration of faith to trust in God: "I will say of the Lord, He is my refuge and my fortress; My God, in Him I will trust." Again, God reminds us of His assurance that He was Jay's refuge in the war zone just as He is our refuge in these moments. We all will have these moments, but God's promise of refuge gives us peace while we are in it. This does not make sense in our natural state of mind but the peace of God that is enabled by the Holy Spirit exceeds our natural understanding. My prayer for Robert and Erick is that God protect and keep them safe from the battles within and to use the principles presented in this book to help them in their journey moving forward.

So what do we do with the battles within as I stated earlier? The battles we face internally are just as real as the physical battles. For Robert and Erick and fellow veterans who are struggling, your friends who helped you would want you to keep fighting as they did for you and not to give up. You don't have to carry the heavy weight of guilt and burden alone because you are not alone. Please seek professional counseling to help successfully navigate this journey. During my army active-duty days, seeking any type of mental help and treatment would not be viewed in a positive manner. It would most likely be viewed as a sign of weakness and not strength. You probably would not want mental treatments documented on your military record. My hope is that the stigma against seeking treatment for mental health is gone in our present time. For any individual to experience this type of trauma in combat, there are going to be some long-term effects on the mental well-being.

I had a heartfelt conversation with my brother-in-law, Leonard E. Johnson, shortly after his retirement from the Philadelphia police department. Officer Johnson was a decorated police officer who served for over thirty years. During his time, he told me many experiences that were traumatizing. As a first responder, he was first many times to the most horrific traffic accidents and first on the scene with house fires before fire fighters arrived and many other life-threatening incidents. During one of those events, he encountered a man with a gun and was shot. He was shot in the vest but still wounded and was knocked to the ground. As Officer Johnson was attempting to recover, he heard the man say, "Today you will die." As the man fired his weapon, it jammed, and Officer Johnson was able to return fire subduing him. Officer Johnson had to eventually get treatment for posttraumatic stress disorder (PTSD). I am sure many of our veterans along with first responders face the same challenges. This is not a badge of shame but a real condition that must be treated.

We get help for physical ailments and diseases, so we must address the mental just as well with the same level of attention without the stigma attached. There is no stigma attached to cancer treatments as I am a cancer survivor, by God's grace, so there should be no stigma attached to seeking treatment for mental illness regardless of the line of work or life circumstance. Our individual pride should not get in the way of our healing.

I will never claim to be an expert in writing about the battles within, but only from what I experienced. I would also offer to our veterans and those that struggle an "anchor of the soul." I have tried to establish that God is trustworthy as the third factor that empowers enduring hope. Here is another view to prove God's trustworthiness. When God made the promise to Abraham in Genesis 22:17 by saying, "Blessing I will bless you, multiplying I will multiply your dependents as the stars of the heaven and as the sand which is on the seashore; and your descendants shall possess the gate of their enemies." He swore by His own name in verse 16. There is no other higher name than Himself. The two things that are unchanging in Genesis are God's promise and His oath. The writer of Hebrews says, "Thus God, determining to show more abundantly to the heirs of promise the immutability of His counsel, confirmed it by an oath" (Hebrews 6:17). An oath was made for Abraham's and our benefit, for His word is eternal, and it is impossible for God to lie. The word *immutability* means unchangeable or unchangeability. In Hebrews 6:19–20, the writer describes this hope we have that is secure in the trustworthiness of God. When we establish contracts for services and the contract is signed by the contractor and the customer receiving the service, the agreement is binding. An honorable contract is the authority that holds the agreement together. We know that sometimes contracts are not honored and broken by men, but we have the hope of God's Word that is unchanging, secure, and eternal. This is the hope that we are able to stand on. We stand on the promises of God that are unchanging, secure, and eternal. The Hebrew writer says, "This hope we have as an anchor of the soul, both sure and steadfast, and which enters the Presence behind the veil."

Why would this be an anchor of the soul? The writer of Hebrews expresses the hope as an anchor of the soul in two ways that is both sure and steadfast. First, the hope is expressed as a ship's anchor. The ship's anchor, even in ancient times, serves the same purpose as today. The ship's anchor is no good unless connected by a chain that connects to the ship preventing it from drifting away into the sea. The audience reading the writing in the first century would fully comprehend the concept of holding the vessel steady and securely in place. Secondly, the writer of the book of Hebrews takes the concept of the anchor of the soul from the ship's harbor to the "Presence behind the vail." So what does this mean? This hope leads us through the curtain of heaven into God's inner sanctuary. The inner sanctuary refers to the most holy place in the Jewish temple. A curtain hung across the entrance to this room, preventing anyone from entering the interior of the most holy place where God resided among His people. The high priest would enter there only once a year (on the Day of Atonement) to stand before God's presence and atone for the sins of the entire nation.

When Jesus decided to die on the cross, a marvelous thing happened for our benefit. We no longer need an earthly high priest to stand before God's presence to atone for sin. But Jesus has already gone there for us, opening the way into God's presence by his death on the cross. His death tore the curtain in two in the temple (Mark 15:38) that separated the interior of the most holy place where God resided. This allows every believer direct access to God. Jesus is an anchor of the soul. He opens the way into God's presence by his death on the cross and on the third day rose again from the dead and now sits on the right hand of the throne of God. Jesus provides the lifeline like the anchor to the ship to hold it steady and secure. Just like the ship that would still be subject to harsh waves of the sea while anchored, we too will experience struggle and harshness that life brings. There must first be a decision to follow Jesus Christ and yield our lives to Him. Jesus is an Anchor of the soul when we want to drift into hopelessness. He is an Anchor of the soul when the mind drifts to have thoughts of suicide. He keeps us from drifting even in the middle of our struggles, which seems like raging storms in a sea. The anchor of the soul works with first a relationship with Jesus Christ and, second, faith in the promises of His word which is secure, unchangeable, and eternal. This is hope that endures and hope that is eternal. I am reminded of how the prophet Isaiah portrays the assuredness of God's word:

> For as the rain comes down, and the snow from heaven, And do not return there, But water the earth, And make it bring forth and bud, That it may give seed to the sower And bread to the eater, So shall My word be that goes forth from My mouth; It shall not return to Me void, But it shall accomplish what I please, And it shall prosper in the thing for which I sent it. (Isaiah 55:10–11)

Just as the cycle of the weather provides for our benefit according to His creation, so shall God's Word achieve its purpose for our benefit according to His will. With this assuredness, be determined and proactive to seek the hope of God that is before us. Jesus promised that He will be with us always, so I am confident with this hope that our hope is enduring.

The Shaping of Purpose

There is a cultural perspective that as we get older, and we begin to change in later years that usefulness and purpose wades. In my younger years, I ran about a six-minute mile, but nowadays, I am happy to be able to move. Yes, we must work through health challenges as we age, but God has designed us with value and purpose in mind that takes us throughout life. Remember how God treasured us in the beginning of life: "For You formed my inward parts; You covered me in my mother's womb I will praise You, for I am fearfully and wonderfully made; Marvelous are Your works, And that my soul knows very well" (Psalms 139:13–14).

God treasures us at the beginning of life and throughout our lives, and He is deliberate in shaping us for His purpose if we allow Him. It is wonderful to know that God values us, regardless of circumstance or where life may take us. This is unchanging! Remember the immutability of God—He is unchanging. Presented in another way in the New Testament the apostle Paul wrote, "For we are His workmanship, created in Christ Jesus for good works, which God prepared beforehand that we should walk in them" (Ephesians 2:10).

Good works reflects what God has designed and purposed us to do. In chapter 1, I quoted Rick Warren's book, *The Purpose Driven Life*, to highlight that we are created for God's purpose, and until we understand this, life will never make sense. Rick Warren further discusses a concept that he describes as SHAPE: "Whenever God gives us an assignment, he always equips us with what we need to accomplish it. This custom combination of capabilities is called your SHAPE: Spiritual gifts, Heart, Abilities Personality and Experience."[23]

So how does the shaping of purpose come together for us? I believe the concept of SHAPE that Rick Warren describes corresponds to God's sovereign plan for our lives. For God's plan to mean anything to us, there must first be a relationship with Jesus Christ; otherwise, nothing in this discussion will fit or make sense. In chapter 1, I presented that "God is sovereign" as the second factor that empowers enduring hope. Admittedly, I spent some effort to explain how suffering as a part of our human experience ties to the sovereignty of God. For many of us this is the most difficult to understand and comprehend, but at the same time, we must understand that God will use those difficult experiences to strengthen us and minister to other people who are suffering. I explained in chapter 1 that the sovereignty of God is a theological term that refers to the unlimited power of God, who has sovereign control over the affairs of nature and history. God's involvement in our human experience is comprehensive and entails every aspect of life. Within God's sovereignty is another theological term called providence. *Providence* means that continuous activity of God whereby He makes all the events of the physical, mental, and moral realms work out His purpose.[24]

There are two major decisions that we all must make when it comes to God's purpose for us. I believe we forfeit fulfillment in life when we do not seek God's purpose. So we must first actively seek God's purpose for our lives. This is an individual choice to recognize God's providence in the shaping of purpose. This shaping involves but not limited to our personalities, all our experiences to include difficult circumstances, losses and sicknesses, education, passion, talents, and gifts. I am using the Rick Warren's concept of SHAPE to highlight how God in His sovereignty will put all this together in

---

[23] Rick Warren, *The Purpose Driven Life: What On Earth Am I Here For?* (Grand Rapids, Zondervan, 2012), 301.

[24] Henry C. Thiessen, *Lectures in Systematic Theology* (Grand Rapids: William B. Eerdmans Publishing Company, 1997), 122.

shaping us for His purpose. In other words, He forms the total person that includes all the elements of life. We may be tempted to put some experiences of our past in the hidden corners of our minds, but God just may have a purpose for your experience to be encouragement and strength for someone else that's on the edge of giving up on life. Ask God to help you see purpose from your SHAPE. We may not see how God is shaping us when we are in the moment of our circumstances, but with the understanding that we are "His workmanship," we can live with the hope that the experience will work out for our good and for the good of others.

We know that Satan and his demons have entered creation; but the enemy, in no way, will stop the plan of God. Therefore, we can live with confidence that nothing will stop God's purpose for us. We will learn from family, teachers, and mentors that we may emulate; but the purpose that God has for us is uniquely ours. The second decision along with actively seeking God's purpose for our lives is to put it into practice or simply live it. Sometimes human expectation may get in the way of seeking God's purpose and putting it into practice. When we think we know how and what direction that God is going to take us, we may occasionally miss the mark. And the enemy will throw roadblocks and obstacles in the way but again he in no way will ever stop God's plan and purpose for us. To be successful, I believe Jesus gave us this simple and profound command: "But seek first the kingdom of God and His righteousness, and all these things shall be added to you" (Matthew 6:33).

This command is simple yet very comprehensive in Matthew chapter 6. It is also recorded in Luke 12:31. It is comprehensive in that it encompasses the discourse that Jesus is teaching covering giving to the needy, prayer and fasting, how to handle money and how not to worry and be distracted by it. But in this single verse, God presents priorities for us in two parts.

First Jesus says, "But seek first the Kingdom of God." This means my life choices and decisions are made with the kingdom of God in mind. This will impact my goals, money management, careers, marriage, pleasures, and other desires. Seeking first the kingdom of God will place these major areas of life in proper priority so that God comes first when considering life decisions. The choices then are made with God guiding our pathway. You might say, "What about the mess I made of my life and the things that are all jumbled up?" There is no better time to start than now. No matter how old you are or where you may find yourself in life, you can use this principle to seek first the kingdom of God to give God priority in your life. I do not speak from a position of perfection, and none of us can. Remember, I am a member of the mistake-makers club and by His grace striving to be like Jesus Christ. You can probably see how God can easily be bumped to second place if we are not actively seeking to put Him first. The word *seek* means to seek after, aim, or strive after. This would imply a continuous activity. We must ask ourselves, are we acknowledging and seeking Him through prayer and meditation on His word when making life choices that He may direct our paths? Are we striving to make the kingdom of God a priority in our lives? Making God a priority in our lives does not limit who you are or lessens opportunities in life but allows you to thrive according to God's purpose and maximize opportunities. Jesus said, "The thief does not come except to steal, and to kill, and to destroy. I come that they may have life, and that they may have it more abundantly" (John 10:10). This is His promise toward us.

The second part in setting our priorities according to this verse is "His righteousness." So we seek first both the kingdom of God and His righteousness as the second part of God's priorities for our lives. The word *righteousness* refers to character or godly character that should reflect how we live. As we put God first above all else, we live righteously as both parts are inseparable. Do not think for one moment that there will not be challenges in following Jesus's command to us. There will be trials and obstacles placed in our way, but when we seek God first, He will enable us to see opportunities even in the obstacles set before us. The last statement in this verse, Jesus said, "And all these things shall be added to you." What are the things He is referring to?

The context suggests these are the very practical things of life that we need. All of us desire and need the necessities of life to include food, clothing, and shelter. The idea is that we don't get caught up in worrying and disturbed about what we need. So Jesus's words at the next verse tells us, "Therefore do not worry or take no thought about tomorrow, for tomorrow will worry about its own things" (Matthew 6:34a). By seeking God first, the things that we need will come as a matter of course because God already knows we need them. For those who have the financial means, these worries of necessities of life may not be an issue at all. However, the same Greek verb phrase used in Matthew's writing "take no thought" is used by Paul in Philippians 4:6. The wording is interpreted as "not be anxious" or not to worry about anything," but by prayer and supplication, make your request known to God with thanksgiving. This command to "not be anxious" is inclusive of every facet of life regardless of need or financial status. The apostle Paul is teaching that the antidote to counteract anxiety and worry is to be prayerful about everything. This is a wonderful scripture that I used in several life applications in this book. I encourage you to abide in it for strength and stability.

As we move forward, it is important to understand that God is deliberate in shaping us for purpose. We must actively seek God's purpose for our lives and then put it into practice while making Him your first priority. As with every concept discussed in this book, I am intentional in relating a biblical illustration to highlight key points. The story of Joseph in the Old Testament is an excellent example of the shaping of purpose. Joseph is recorded as being seventeen years old as his story begins. Joseph alienated his brothers by bringing a bad report to their father, Jacob (Genesis 37:2). Jacob loved Joseph more than all his children because he was the son of his old age, and he made him a tunic of many colors (robe). The significance of this is that it continued to show favor toward Joseph and stirred anger, jealousy, and hatred with his brothers. This would perhaps be a recipe for disaster for any family. What we will observe in this story is God's providence in each difficult episode of Joseph's life and proving the three factors that empowers enduring hope: God is the object of our hope, God is sovereign, and God is trustworthy.

As a young seventeen-year-old, God gave Joseph a gift to dream and interpret dreams. He had two dreams involving him and his family. The dreams appeared to show a relationship of authority over his family. Perhaps due to his young age and immaturity, Joseph showed little skill in communicating this sensitive subject to his brothers and his parents. He wasted no time to tell the first dream to his brothers:

> "Listen to this dream," he said. "We were out in the field, tying up bundles of grain. Suddenly my bundle stood up, and your bundles all gathered around and bowed low before mine!" His brothers responded, "So you think you will be our king, do you? Do you actually think you will reign over us?" And they hated him all the more because of his dreams and the way he talked about them. (Genesis 37:6–8 NLT)

The relationship between Joseph and his brothers was already very strained because of the favored relationship with Jacob. Showing little tack and perhaps a little arrogance, Joseph dreamed for the second time and again wasted no time telling his brothers, "Soon Joseph had another dream, and again he told his brothers about it. Listen, I have had another dream, he said. "The sun, moon, and eleven stars bowed low before me!" (Genesis 37:9 NLT).

This time, he also told his father Jacob of his dreams, and he scolded him. His father questioned Joseph as to what kind of dreams is this "that your parents and brothers would actually come and bow before you?" While his brothers' heart was hardened with hatred and jealousy, his father Jacob kept the matter within himself and perhaps pondered the meaning.

On an occasion, when his brothers were feeding the flock near Shechem—an ancient, fortified city in central Palestine and important place in the religious history of the Hebrew people—Jacob instructed Joseph to check on the well-being of his brothers and the flock and bring back word to him. With a reputation of giving a bad report to the father and among the dreams, the brothers were not happy to see Joseph. The brothers seeing him from a distance, they conspired against him to kill him and dump him into a pit (Genesis 37:18–20). But one of the brothers, Reuben, heard their murderous intent and decided he would deliver Joseph out of their hands. Reuben told the brothers not to kill him but leave him in the pit, and they agreed. Reuben's intent was to go back later and retrieve Joseph and return him to Jacob. The brothers stripped Joseph of his tunic of many colors and dumped him into a pit.

Then afterward they sat down to have lunch. It is rather unimaginable that the hardness of their hearts was to the extent that they would take time to have lunch while this young seventeen-year-old was cast into a deep hole. Although Reuben had intentions of retrieving him later, this was still terrifying for young Joseph. Later in this biblical narrative, the brothers will acknowledge the anguish of Joseph's soul when he pleaded with them, and they ignored his distress recorded in Genesis 42:21. As this difficult and threatening situation unfolds, God's providence is at work as He is allowing the events to take place according to His purpose for Joseph. Joseph was not killed but kept alive at the insisting of Reuben. The brothers looked up as they were eating and noticed a caravan of Ishmaelites (also called Midianites) traders carrying spices, balm, and myrrh heading to Egypt. This was typical traffic for where they were located. The chief articles of commerce were these species and aromatic materials. The balm or "balm of Gilead" was renowned for its medical qualities. The brothers decided it would be better to sell Joseph to the Ishmaelites instead of killing him. So as the caravan was passing by, they pulled Joseph out of the pit and sold him to the Ishmaelites for twenty shekels of silver, and they took Joseph to Egypt (Genesis 37:26–28). It is apparent from this biblical narrative that slaves were also part of the Ishmaelites' articles of commerce. Reuben was not present when Joseph was sold into slavery. Joseph's brothers decided to deceive their father by taking his tunic and killing a goat, dipping the tunic in the goat's blood to convince Jacob that Joseph was killed by a wild beast (Genesis 37:31–33).

It is easy for us to look at biblical history to see God's providence in the events of Joseph's life. We can look ahead and see that Joseph will be essential for survival of the Hebrew nation who facilitated Jacob's eventual move to Egypt along with seventy members of his extended family. The descendants of Jacob will grow into a mighty nation in Egypt until the appointed time that God delivered them out of the land recorded in Exodus. The Bible says, "But the children of Israel were fruitful and increased abundantly, multiplied and grew exceedingly mighty; and the land was filled with them" (Exodus 1:7).

But now at the present time, at seventeen, Joseph was taken captive and headed to Egypt as a slave. He could not see thirteen years ahead of his life as we can in this biblical narrative. Right now, Joseph is experiencing great despair in his life. Suddenly taken away from him was his youth, relationship with his father, freedom, sense of security, and identity. This was abruptly taken from him by the hands of his brothers. Perhaps he did not realize the extent of their hatred for him, but it manifested before him suddenly and harshly. This is a traumatic event that would impact anyone long term, but despite the extreme circumstance, I believe there was enough awareness of God's presence within Joseph that will carry him through what is seemingly an uncertain future. As God works through each difficult episode, He proved that He is with Joseph and is sovereignly in control.

> Now Joseph had been taken down to Egypt. And Potiphar, an officer of Pharaoh, captain of the guard, an Egyptian, bought him from the Ishmaelites who had taken him down there. The Lord was with Joseph, and he was a successful man; and he was in the house of his master the Egyptian. And his master saw that the Lord was with him and that the Lord made all he did to prosper in his hand. So Joseph found favor in his sight, and served him. Then he made him overseer of his house, and all that he had he put under his authority. So it was, from the time that he had made him overseer of his house and all that he had, that the Lord blessed the Egyptian's house for Joseph's sake; and the blessing of the Lord was on all that he had in the house and in the field. Thus he left all that he had in Joseph's hand, and

he did not know what he had except for the bread
which he ate. (Genesis 39:1–6)

The scripture does not give a sense of time, but there was enough time to find favor with Potiphar, to learn the Egyptian language and customs. It was enough time needed for Joseph to be successful, for Potiphar to see that the Lord was with Joseph and that everything Joseph did prosper. The prosperity of Potiphar's house was through Joseph, and he made him overseer of his estate. Joseph's stewardship of the Egyptian household was to the extent that Potiphar did not worry about anything except what kind of food to eat. This is significant trust given to Joseph. There were other servants working in the Egyptian house, and we can assume that Joseph had administrative oversight to manage their affairs. The scripture is clear that the Lord was with Joseph and the primary driver for his success. But with this, Joseph had to make some critical choices that were essential to him moving forward at this stage of his life. He could have allowed his perspective to be back at the pit and his situation as a slave to shape his attitude toward Potiphar and those around him. Joseph had to choose to make the best of what was given him. There is no doubt that what his brothers did to him was still very vivid in his memory, but it did not hinder him from giving his best in a difficult situation, and God provided the increase.

God can use us when we are willing vessels for him and not allow despair to overshadow our awareness of the God that is within us. It is possible that even in a harsh and toxic work environment, God will give you favor when we are totally submitted to Him, and He continues to be the object of our hope. I am reminded of the advice that the apostle Paul gave to servants:

> Bondservants, obey in all things your masters according to the flesh, not with eyeservice, as men-pleasers, but in sincerity of heart, fearing God. And whatever you do, do it heartily, as to the Lord and not to men, knowing that from the Lord you will receive the reward of the inheri-

tance; for you serve the Lord Christ. (Colossians
3:22–24)

Paul's advice is very valid in our work environment today. Replace the word *servant*, which means slave with employee. It is simple: "Whatever you do, do it heartily, as to the Lord and not to man." When we give our best as employees and employers as unto to God, we give Him the opportunity to provide the increase for us. This means to put our focus on God and less on the frustrations of people. Making this commitment unto God entails acknowledging Him in our decisions and working solutions in the work process. God honors faithfulness and will provide for your success as you give your best as unto the Lord. This is not an easy pill but a walk of faith that allows God to guide your pathway even in a difficult and toxic work environment. Potiphar was able to see Joseph giving his best and the evidence of God blessing his estate.

So Joseph is doing his best and God is blessing Potiphar's house, but his wife now takes notice of Joseph. The scripture says that "Joseph was handsome in form and appearance." One translation added "very handsome and well-built young man." Mrs. Potiphar's attention to Joseph turned into a lustful pursuit and pressured him to go to bed with her. Joseph refused and his response against her advances reflects godly character even in the midst of a very difficult and awkward circumstance that would have easily been the demise of other biblical characters including his brothers. The pivotal declaration of Joseph's character is his response:

> But he refused and said to his master's wife, "Look, my master does not know what is with me in the house, and he has committed all that he has to my hand. There is no one greater in this house than I, nor has he kept back anything from me but you, because you are his wife. How then can I do this great wickedness, and sin against God?" (Genesis 39:8–9)

Consider Joseph's response: "How then can I do this great wickedness and sin against God?" He respected Potiphar, but he was not so much concerned about Potiphar's reaction but that of his faithfulness to God. He was not concerned about Mrs. Potiphar's feelings, but clearly, God was at the forefront. There was no question that the righteousness of God was first in Joseph's mind. Potiphar's wife continued to pursue Joseph day by day, but he refused her advances to sleep with her. One day she made sure no other servants were in the house, and when Joseph went in to do his work, she grabbed him by his garment saying, "Lie with me." But he left his garment in her hand and fled and ran outside. Making God first in our living means putting action to our words. Joseph knew he could not stay in that situation particularly sexual temptation. The outcome may have been different if he stayed. Potiphar's wife falsely accused Joseph of sexual assault. She told the false accusation to the men in the house that Joseph came into lie with her, and when she cried out with a loud voice, he fled, leaving his garment in her hand. She kept the garment and waited until Potiphar came home. There were no other witnesses to counter or collaborate her story. But scripture will prove that God was with Joseph. In this no-win situation, God was in the midst shaping and preparing Joseph for what's to come.

> So it was, when his master heard the words which his wife spoke to him, saying, "Your servant did to me after this manner," that his anger was aroused. Then Joseph's master took him and put him into the prison, a place where the king's prisoners were confined. And he was there in the prison. But the Lord was with Joseph and showed him mercy, and He gave him favor in the sight of the keeper of the prison. (Genesis 39:19–21)

Joseph's story now moves swiftly into a worse condition. He is moved from being the chief steward of a wealthy Egyptian household to prison. For many of us going from bad to worse, we may question God and ponder why He allowed this. I believe Joseph was a regular person just like anyone else—he was not divine and given super-natural power beyond human ability. But he was a young man with incredible integrity and trust in God. Joseph, at this point, could not phantom what is ahead, but he had the same perspective that prevailed while he was a slave at Potiphar's house and the Lord was with him and he prospered even while in the dungeon.

> And the keeper of the prison committed to Joseph's hand all the prisoners who were in the prison; whatever they did there, it was his doing. The keeper of the prison did not look into anything that was under Joseph's authority, because the Lord was with him; and whatever he did, the Lord made it prosper. (Genesis 39:22–23)

Joseph was placed where the king's prisoners were confined. At some point, Pharoah's chief butler and chief baker offended Pharaoh, and both men were committed to the same prison with Joseph. Scripture do not reveal what offended Pharaoh, but both men were highly trusted in his court. The captain of the guard put Joseph in charge of them, and he served them for an unspecified time. It is important to note Joseph was in position to serve these men. Sometimes in our most dreadful moments, God may use us to serve others in their circumstances, but we must trust Him at every step as Joseph did at each dreadful episode. Both men had dreams that troubled them and each with their own meaning. When Joseph noticed their sad expressions and questioned what was wrong, they told him about their dreams. Joseph was aware of his gifts of dreams, but at this point, he is now able to offer interpretation. He acknowledged to the chief butler and baker that interpretation belongs to God and asked them to tell him their dreams. It is important to note that Joseph gave credit to God and not himself. So the chief butler told Joseph his dream.

> And Joseph said to him, "This is the interpretation of it: The three branches are three days.

> Now within three days Pharaoh will lift up your head and restore you to your place, and you will put Pharaoh's cup in his hand according to the former manner, when you were his butler. (Genesis 40:12–13)

When Joseph gave the interpretation, he made a specific request in verses 14–15 for the chief butler to remember him, to put in a good word to Pharaoh and get him out. This is the only time recorded that Joseph makes a specific request on his behalf. Joseph told the chief butler that he was stolen away from his homeland and have done nothing that would warrant being placed into the dungeon. Is Joseph complaining? No, this was a reasonable request of someone who was wrongfully accused. Many of us perhaps would be complaining on day 1 and asserting our innocence to the authorities, but no indication from Joseph. He continued to trust the sovereign God in his circumstance. The chief butler is one of the closest people to Pharaoh in his inner court and would not require a special summons or meeting. Now as this narrative continues, the chief baker observed that Joseph's interpretation was good and told Joseph how his dream unfolded.

> When the chief baker saw that the interpretation was good, he said to Joseph, "I also was in my dream, and there were three white baskets on my head. In the uppermost basket were all kinds of baked goods for Pharaoh, and the birds ate them out of the basket on my head." So Joseph answered and said, "This is the interpretation of it: The three baskets are three days. Within three days Pharaoh will lift off your head from you and hang you on a tree; and the birds will eat your flesh from you." (Genesis 40:16–19)

This was not the outcome that the chief baker was looking for. Joseph was a man of integrity and gave the accurate interpretation of the chief baker's dream. The temptation would have been to give the chief baker a better-sounding outcome but remember the interpretations were of God not of Joseph. In three days on an occasion of Pharaoh's birthday, he made feasts for all his servants. He restored the chief butler to his former position, but he hanged the chief baker just as Joseph had interpreted to them. However, the chief butler did not remember Joseph. Joseph was left in prison for two years. How simple would it be for the chief butler to remember Joseph and put in a positive word for him to Pharaoh? Scripture does not record Joseph's reaction, but humanly speaking, this was probably devastating for him and would put many of us in a state of disillusionment. When it comes to this level of disillusionment and pain, Dr. Charles Swindoll gives this advice:

> We have two choices: We can become disillusioned and embittered, or we can use that difficulty as a platform for putting our hope and trust in the living God. Disillusionment is a dangerous, slippery slope. First, we become disillusioned about our fellow man. Then we move on to cynicism. Before long, we trust no one, not even God. We've been burned. We've been taken advantage of; we've been mistreated. I have never met an individual who was truly disillusioned with mankind who has not also become disillusioned with God. The two go together. Cynicism is pawned in such a context.[25]

But for this remarkable young man, the scripture gives no indication of his disillusionment and distrust of God and people. I can only make assumptions about what he may have felt during this time. What was it like for Joseph as he waited? What were his thoughts and questions toward God? The Genesis account gives no details except

---

[25] Dr. Charles R. Swindoll, *Joseph: A Man of Integrity and Forgiveness* (Nashville, Word Publishing, 1998), 52.

that the chief butler did not remember Joseph. I would hold that Joseph maintained his trust in the living God in the midst of his pain. Maintaining our faith and trust in God would not only help us go through step-by-step and day by day in our situation but prepare us to move to the next step according to God's purpose. Joseph could have allowed bitterness, disillusionment, and cynicism to consume him but allowed God to keep his mind and walk in the assurance that the Lord was with him. If Joseph degenerated into a total state of distrust toward God and people, he would not be in position to be used by God at the next critical point in his journey. In the next life-changing event in Joseph's journey, we shall see why this was so critical.

As the story continued, Pharaoh had two troubling dreams. He could not understand the dreams recorded in Genesis 41:1–7 and called for the magicians and wise men of Egypt to interpret, but they could not offer interpretations of his dreams. Pharaoh dreamed that he was standing on the riverbank and observed seven fat, healthy cows coming out of the river and began grazing in the marsh grass. Pharaoh then observed seven more cows coming up behind them, but these were gaunt and ugly in appearance. The gaunt and ugly cows stood beside the seven fat and healthy cows and ate them. Pharaoh then woke up from his dream. Perhaps not giving much thought about what this meant except very unusual, he fell asleep again and had a second dream. In this second dream, he saw seven heads of grain, plump and good. Then he noticed seven more heads of grain, but those were shriveled and withered by the wind. The shriveled and withered heads of grain swallowed up the plump and good heads. Pharaoh then woke up again and realized it was a dream.

When the magicians and all the wise men of Egypt failed to give interpretation to Pharaoh of these troubling dreams, the chief butler spoke to Pharaoh that he remembered his faults that landed him and the chief baker in prison and that they both had dreams, and each had a meaning of its own. He told Pharaoh of Joseph, a young Hebrew who was the servant of the captain of the guard that he interpreted their dreams. The events from their dreams turned out exactly as he said. He was restored to his former position as the chief butler, and the chief baker was executed as Joseph predicted. After hearing this, Pharaoh sent for Joseph and he was quickly brought from the dungeon to stand before Pharaoh.

Prior to standing before Pharaoh, Joseph shaved and changed his clothes. I can imagine at this point that he was bearded and wearing prison attire but made himself more presentable before the king. He could not imagine what was ahead but had a mind that was prepared for what God had next. It is amazing how this story quickly turns in another direction. It is important to remember that God's timing is not our timing. Joseph was left abandoned in the dungeon for two years, yet his trust in God remained intact and not overcome by bitterness. I believe many times we need to pray for God to keep our minds during times of trouble.

The apostle Paul advised young Timothy when facing severe persecution as a church leader that "God has not given us a spirit of fear, but of power and of love and of a sound mind" (2 Timothy 1:7). The sound mind refers to discipline and self-control. When we are tempted to lose control, pray for God's keeping power to hold us together. The same God that kept Joseph will keep us in time of trouble, abandonment, hatred, and abuse. Our faith must triumph over our fears and our trials. Beyond Pharaoh, Joseph was prepared to move with God when He determined the time to move. Pharaoh's dreams were by divine providence and God has shaped Joseph through each difficult episode of his life for such a time as this.

So Joseph came to Pharaoh, and he told Joseph about his dreams and there was no one that could interpret it. This implying that none of the wisest men in Egypt could interpret his dreams except for what he heard about Joseph's interpretations of the chief butler and chief baker's dreams. So Joseph replied to Pharaoh, "It is not in me; God will give Pharaoh an answer of peace" (Genesis 41:16).

There was no element of pride or boasting in Joseph's answer to Pharaoh, but he gave God glory for what he was about to do, and God clearly was at the forefront before Pharaoh. Since Joseph put God at the forefront and not himself, God will be the source of Pharaoh's desire for peace and comfort from these disturbing and troubling dreams. So Pharaoh told his two dreams to Joseph, and then he gave the interpretation:

> Then Joseph said to Pharaoh, "The dreams of Pharaoh are one; God has shown Pharaoh what He is about to do: The seven good cows are seven years, and the seven good heads are seven years; the dreams are one. And the seven thin and ugly cows which came up after them are seven years, and the seven empty heads blighted by the east wind are seven years of famine. This is the thing which I have spoken to Pharaoh. God has shown Pharaoh what He is about to do. Indeed, seven years of great plenty will come throughout all the land of Egypt but after them seven years of famine will arise, and all the plenty will be forgotten in the land of Egypt; and the famine will deplete the land. So, the plenty will not be known in the land because of the famine following, for it will be very severe. And the dream was repeated to Pharaoh twice because the thing is established by God, and God will shortly bring it to pass." (Genesis 41:25–32)

Joseph was able to show Pharaoh what God is about to do over the next fourteen years with seven years of great plenty and prosperity followed by seven years of famine. The famine years will be so severe that the years of plenty will be forgotten. God is at the center of these dreams and had decreed that they will shortly come to pass by Joseph's interpretation. In addition to the interpretation of Pharaoh's dreams, Joseph gave him an implementation plan for the next fourteen years so that the nation does not go into ruin. Joseph advises Pharaoh to appoint a wise and intelligent overseer to put him in charge over the land and then let him appoint commissioners to collect one-fifth of the produce during the plentiful years and store as reserves in the cities under the authority of Pharaoh.

Joseph not only provided the interpretation of Pharaoh's dreams but also offered a wise plan critical for the survival of the nation. Notice again there was no boasting or hinting that he would be the person to oversee this plan or be involved in any way but rather a humble perspective to suggest solutions to what God decreed through Pharaoh's dreams. Joseph's response to Pharaoh is also a reflection of his awareness and confidence in his gifting from God in organizational and leadership skills that were evident at Potiphar's household as his chief steward and as the servant of the captain of the guard. Joseph was willing to do his best and use his gifts regardless of his circumstance and God provided the increase. God in His sovereignty has given each individual natural talents when we are born into this world, and when we come into relationship with him through Jesus Christ, he has also given us spiritual gifts. God will use them together for his glory and to assist others. Now, Joseph's journey continues with Pharaoh's response:

> So, the advice was good in the eyes of Pharaoh and in the eyes of all his servants. And Pharaoh said to his servants, "Can we find such a one as this, a man in whom is the Spirit of God?" Then Pharaoh said to Joseph, "Inasmuch as God has shown you all this, there is no one as discerning and wise as you. You shall be over my house, and all my people shall be ruled according to your word; only in regard to the throne will I be greater than you." And Pharaoh said to Joseph, "See, I have set you over all the land of Egypt." Then Pharaoh took his signet ring off his hand and put it on Joseph's hand; and he clothed him in garments of fine linen and put a gold chain around his neck. And he had him ride in the second chariot which he had; and they cried out before him, "Bow the knee!" So, he set him over all the land of Egypt. (Genesis 41:37–43)

This is a major change in Joseph's life who is now thirty years old at this point. It was thirteen years since the time Joseph was sold into slavery. Joseph now stands as a man with great authority, second only to Pharaoh as the governor of Egypt who was charged to not only manage Egypt's preparation and response to famine, but approving authority to surrounding nations who would come to buy grain. I can only imagine how Joseph must have felt as he was suddenly thrust into a high-level position, to ride in the second chariot and his entourage crying out "bow the knee" as he went before the people. Please note again that there was no evidence of boasting or arrogance on Joseph's part. There was no indication of revenge on those who treated him harshly. He handled the elevation in a humbled spirit. Joseph now recognized his position, and every turn of his life was by God's providence and set out to accomplish this extraordinary task that was before him. Pharaoh changed his name to Zaphnath-Paaneah and arranged for him to be given a wife—Asenath, the daughter of Poti-Pherah priest of On and from this union two sons were born. Joseph called the name of his first son "Manasseh" and said, "For God has made me forget all my toil and all my father's house." Joseph named his second son "Ephraim" and said, "For God has caused me to be fruitful in the land of my affliction."

In the Bible, parents would give meaning to the names of their children. The word *toil* associated with his father's house refers to grievance, pain, and trouble. The memory will be there, but I believe God has allowed him to live and move forward without the grievance and pain associated with the memory of his father's house. Joseph has come to the place that he sees God's fruitfulness in the land where he was once a slave. With the major change in Joseph's life, I believe he maintained his trust in the living God and never lost sight of his identity as a man of God. This again would put Joseph in position to move with God in the next juncture in his life. Even Pharaoh recognizes the God in Joseph. "And Pharaoh said to his servants, 'Can we find such a one as this, a man in whom is the Spirit of God?'" (Genesis 41:38).

The Genesis account indicates that Joseph wasted little time to put the plan in place for Egypt's response to the coming famine. Joseph strategically placed food reserves in every city that surrounded the fields. The quantity of the food gathered was significant and described as immeasurable during the first seven years. After the growing and gathering season ended, the land of Egypt was famished, and the people cried out to Pharaoh, and he directed them to Joseph to begin the support plan for the people. At the same time, the famine was severe in the surrounding countries to include his home country of Canaan. At this point, Joseph's father Jacob heard that there was grain in Egypt, and he directed his sons to go buy grain in Egypt or else they die.

> When Jacob saw that there was grain in Egypt, Jacob said to his sons, "Why do you look at one another?" And he said, "Indeed I have heard that there is grain in Egypt; go down to that place and buy for us there, that we may live and not die. So Joseph's ten brothers went down to buy grain in Egypt. But Jacob did not send Joseph's brother Benjamin with his brothers, for he said, "Lest some calamity befall him." (Genesis 42:1–4)

So Jacob's sons journeyed to Egypt to buy grain. All those who would buy grain from Egypt can only come through Joseph. By Pharaoh's decree, "without Joseph's consent, no man may lift his hand or foot in all the land of Egypt." The sons of Jacob came face-to-face to the Governor of Egypt not knowing it was their younger brother Joseph.

> Now Joseph was governor over the land; and it was he who sold to all the people of the land. And Joseph's brothers came and bowed down before him with their faces to the earth. Joseph saw his brothers and recognized them, but he acted as a stranger to them and spoke roughly to them. Then he said to them, "Where do you

come from?" And they said, "From the land of Canaan to buy food. "So, Joseph recognized his brothers, but they did not recognize him. Then Joseph remembered the dreams which he had dreamed about them, and said to them, "You are spies! You have come to see the nakedness of the land!" (Genesis 42:6–9)

Joseph recognized his brothers, but they did not recognize him. He accused them of being spies and spoke roughly to them through an interpreter. As the brothers bowed down before him, the realization of his dreams as a teenager came to light before him. Can you imagine after over twenty years to come face-to-face with those who wanted to kill you and then decided to sell you into slavery. But Joseph maintained his control and kept his identity hidden from his brothers. He continued the accusations that they were spies, but the brothers pleaded that they are honest men consisting of twelve brothers from one man. The youngest brother is with their father and the other is no more.

Joseph decided to imprison them for three days so that their words be tested. After the third day, he instructed them to return to Canaan with the grain for their house and bring back the younger brother Benjamin. One of them would remain in prison until they returned. When Joseph heard them speaking among themselves in their native Hebrew language expressing regret and anguish for what they did to him as a young boy, he understood what they were saying and turned away and wept. He returned to them again and had Simeon imprisoned and the rest of the brothers returned to Canaan with the grain needed to survive.

Bible scholars suggest Joseph was testing his brothers to ensure their honesty and for him to see his younger brother again, which is indicated in verse 16. Perhaps also considering suddenly coming face-to-face with his brothers after so many years, I believe Joseph needed time to process what was happening. The rough speaking and telling them that they were spies possibly served as a cover for what was going on inside of him. Joseph was a great man of integrity, who showed great faith in all the trauma that he faced, but he had the same human emotions and struggles as anyone else. For whatever the reason, to test his brothers or to give himself cover and time to think, God made the provision for Joseph. As God was with Joseph during times of despair, He is with him in a position of authority to work through now the encounter with his brothers. How should we respond in a situation when face-to-face with those who abused us and treated us harshly? The brothers concluded that Joseph was good as dead, not knowing the outcome of being sold into slavery. Ultimately, we respond by giving glory to God and trusting Him by the power of the Holy Spirit. By the power of the Holy Spirit, we hope to maintain control and allow our words to reflect godly character. Joseph's response has been consistent in every episode in his journey, and God continues to shape him according to His purpose.

Joseph's brothers returned to Canaan with the provision of grain. On the way to their encampment as they were feeding their animals, they discovered their money to purchase the grain was returned in their sacks. They all wondered in amazement and their hearts filled with fear and said to each other, "What has God done to us?" They previously acknowledged that the harsh treatment by Joseph as governor of the land was connected to their treatment of him. The brothers were seeing God at work but not comprehending what God was up to. We sometimes conclude that we don't know what God is up to, but we should trust in His plan for us. God is not only shaping Joseph, but his brothers as well. After returning to Canaan, the brothers told their father Jacob the conditions to buy more grain. They must prove their honesty to the governor of Egypt by returning with the younger brother Benjamin and securing the release of Simeon. This arrangement brought great grief and distress to their father Jacob, and he refused. For Jacob, Joseph is dead, and all he has left is the younger brother and the fear of some calamity happening to him would be overwhelming.

> But he said, "My son shall not go down with
> you, for his brother is dead, and he is left alone.
> If any calamity should befall him along the way

in which you go, then you would bring down
my gray hair with sorrow to the grave." (Genesis
42:38)

The famine in Canaan continued in its severity, and Jacob's family ate all the grain they brought from Egypt. Jacob told his sons to go back to Egypt to buy a little more food, but Judah reminded him that they cannot return unless the younger brother is with them. In Jacob's frustration, he could not understand why they told the governor they had another brother. But the brothers also baffled as to why this Egyptian governor was asking pointed questions about their family that they had no choice but to answer.

"But they said, 'The man asked us pointedly about ourselves and our family, saying, "Is your father still alive? Have you another brother?" And we told him according to these words. Could we possibly have known that he would say, "Bring your brother down"?'" (Genesis 43:7).

God works in ways that we will not fully understand. Sometimes we may feel pushed in a corner with few options. Our only choice is to trust God when it is difficult to see and understand His plan. David said in Psalm 139:9–10, "If I take the wings of the morning, and dwell in the uttermost parts of the sea, even there Your hand shall lead me and Your right hand shall hold me." Although in our human experience we may at times feel remote from God and lonely, but He promised His ever presence no matter the circumstance. So we should never distance ourselves from Him. Trust His hand to lead you and His righteous right hand to hold you. What does this look like? It can be as simple as "Lord, I trust You to lead me through this trouble and to hold me together so I don't lose control and fall apart."

Jacob may have felt that in the situation with the famine in Canaan and the prospect of the sons going back to Egypt with is his youngest son Benjamin, he had no good options and perhaps feeling very remote and isolated as to what to do. Jacob, now in an act of faith for God's mercy, realized that it must be so and instructed his sons to return to Egypt and take back the money given them, reasoning that it may have been an oversight. Also, they would take gifts to include a little balm, honey, spices, and myrrh (aromatic gum), pistachio nuts, and almonds. In a famine, these would be precious commodities and also rare in Egypt.

So Jacob's sons traveled to Egypt with Benjamin and the gifts. When they stood before Joseph and he noticed Benjamin was with them, his only instructions to his steward were to prepare a meal for them to dine with him at noon. A stark contrast from the first encounter when Joseph accused them of being spies. The brothers thought because of the money that was in their sacks that Joseph directed them to his palace. When they arrived at the palace, Jacob's sons explained their concerns to the steward, but he assured them that this was not a mistake or that they did anything wrong. The steward brought Simeon out to them who was left in prison waiting for their return. Even this Egyptian recognized that their God was up to something and did not attribute it to anything else!

"But he said, 'Peace be with you, do not be afraid. Your God and the God of your father has given you treasure in your sacks; I had your money.' Then he brought Simeon out to them" (Genesis 43:23).

So the brothers entered Joseph's palace, and the servant prepared them to meet Joseph by washing their feet and giving their animals feed. They were told they would be eating there, so they prepared the gifts from Canaan. When Joseph arrived, they presented the gifts and bowed down before him giving honor. Joseph asked if their father was still alive, and they replied that he was in good health. It was then he noticed his younger brother Benjamin and Joseph asked, "Is this your younger brother?" And he said, "God be gracious to you, my son." Jacob's sons could not imagine the purpose of these questions and perhaps they thought a change in heart from the governor of Egypt. But inside of Joseph were emotions that were overwhelming. It was at this point that he hurried away to his chambers and wept. After he regained control and washed his face, he ordered that the meal be served. To the brothers', amazement each were seated according to their birthright. This could only occur with prior knowledge of the family, but the brothers were clueless.

Jacob's sons and Joseph ate the meal together and would appear to be a pleasant feast. As the brothers were preparing to leave early the next day, Joseph instructed his steward to fill the men's sacks with food and put the money they carried to purchase the food back in their sacks. Joseph also instructed his servant to place his silver cup in Benjamin's sack and follow them as they made their way outside the city. The Egyptians believe that this silver cup is used to predict the future, but Joseph being a man of God had no need beyond what God has revealed to him. Joseph gave his steward specific instructions once he caught up to the brothers.

> As soon as the morning dawned, the men were sent away, they and their donkeys. When they had gone out of the city, and were not yet far off, Joseph said to his steward, "Get up, follow the men; and when you overtake them, say to them, 'Why have you repaid evil for good? Is not this the one from which my lord drinks, and with which he indeed practices divination? You have done evil in so doing.'" (Genesis 44:3–5)

When the steward caught up with them, he spoke to them as Joseph instructed him. When the brothers heard the words of Joseph's steward, they were dismayed at the accusation and responded in disbelief as to how this would be possible. They returned the money to buy food, and it would be unthinkable to steal silver and gold from the governor given the high penalty for doing so. They declared that each man search their sacks with confidence that nothing would be found in their possession. The steward said that whoever has the silver cup shall be his slave and the rest of them shall be blameless. To the brother's amazement, the silver cup was found in Benjamin's sack. The brothers tore their clothing at the revelation. This is a customary Jewish expression of grief and profound sadness. The brothers would not dare return to Canaan without their younger brother, so they packed up and went back to Egypt to face Joseph. Joseph was still at his palace, apparently waiting on the outcome of the encounter between the brothers and the steward.

"And Joseph said to them, 'What deed is this you have done? Did you not know that such a man as I can certainly practice divination?'" (Genesis 44:15).

Judah spoke on behalf of everyone. He had no words to justify their possession of Joseph's cup but would only conclude that they all are guilty and will be his slaves. Joseph's response that this would not be so and only Benjamin who was found with the cup shall be his slave. The next response from Judah is an amazing appeal on behalf of his youngest brother and his father Jacob in Genesis 44:18–34. This is not only a heartfelt appeal on behalf of others but an expression of a contrite-repentant heart. This is the same Judah that also conspired with his brothers to kill Joseph but then decided to cast him into a pit and sold him into slavery. Commentators suggest that this was the final test by Joseph to prove the brothers' honesty.

I have no doubt that with the wisdom Joseph demonstrated in his journey, this would be the case; however, I would also add another possibility. Joseph's heart yearned for his younger brother when he was overcome with emotion and had to steal away before anyone noticed (Genesis 43:30). It is perhaps a possibility that Joseph wanted to get to know his younger brother before the others. But whether this was his test of a changed heart of the brothers or an effort to get more time with his younger brother, God brought about a change in the brother's heart. Although Judah was the spokesperson, I believe the rest were experiencing the change. Ultimately, God presented the condition that touched the hearts of these men that were once so hardened with hate they were willing to kill Joseph. It was their choice to be of a repentant heart. Judah appealed to Joseph to let the younger brother go free and take him as a slave instead and let him go home with the rest of the brothers. Judah offering his life for his younger brother is clearly evident of a changed heart.

What happens next is an amazing turn in Joseph's journey. I don't believe Joseph could have anticipated the sincere appeal from Judah on behalf of Benjamin and his father Jacob. For the first time, there was expression of concern for Jacob's well-being in that if they returned to Canaan without Benjamin, Jacob would be overcome with grief and die. This moved Joseph to the point that he could not restrain himself any longer. He had to reveal to these brothers that "I am Joseph."

> Then Joseph could not restrain himself before all those who stood by him, and he cried out, "Make everyone go out from me!" So, no one stood with him while Joseph made himself known to his brothers. And he wept aloud, and the Egyptians and the house of Pharaoh heard it. Then Joseph said to his brothers, "I am Joseph; does my father still live?" But his brothers could not answer him, for they were dismayed in his presence. And Joseph said to his brothers, "Please come near to me." So, they came near. Then he said: "I am Joseph your brother, whom you sold into Egypt. But now, do not therefore be grieved or angry with yourselves because you sold me here; for God sent me before you to preserve life. For these two years the famine has been in the land, and there are still five years in which there will be neither plowing nor harvesting. And God sent me before you to preserve a posterity for you in the earth, and to save your lives by a great deliverance. So now it was not you who sent me here, but God; and He has made me a father to Pharaoh, and lord of all his house, and a ruler throughout all the land of Egypt. (Genesis 45:1–8)

Joseph now reveals himself to his brothers and they stood still in shock. They knew by the unusual nature that the governor was asking pointed questions about their father and if there was another brother that something was happening. When they discovered all the money they had to purchase grain after the first trip was returned, they questioned, "What has God done to us?" This may have indicated that something unusual was happening. The response of Joseph's steward at the palace when the brothers expressed their concerns may have provided a clue that something unusual was happening in their favor, but they could not have imagined this! The words "I am Joseph" put the brothers in such a state of paralysis they could not respond. Joseph told them to please come near him. This was more of an affectionate request and not an authoritative request. Joseph knew that the realization of who he is and the position that he now holds may have put terror in the older brother's mind. Then he gives them the assurance to not be grieved and even angry with themselves because of the horrible act of hatred they committed against him. Joseph words of assurance would not be possible if he had not first forgiven his brothers. I believe Joseph forgave his brothers prior to the feast at the palace. His response to these men was an act of grace, which was more than they could have imagined. He did not hold the past against them.

The act of forgiveness is not always easy to achieve. This is not done on your own strength, but by the power of the Holy Spirit. The word of God told us, "And whenever you stand praying, if you have anything against anyone, forgive him that your Father in heaven may also forgive you your trespasses" (Mark 11:25). Forgiveness is the act of pardoning someone for their wrong, trespasses, injustice against us despite their shortcomings and faults. We no longer hold grudges and hatred. We must give that over to God to help us. God will not give us a command without giving us the power to perform. Joseph forgiving his brothers may not have been sudden, but God has given him what he needed to do His will.

The shaping of purpose for Joseph was deliberate by the sovereign God. Him being sold into slavery brought him to Egypt. The time spent at Potiphar's house as his chief steward provided the means to get accustomed to the country and sharpened organization skills. The false accusation of sexual assault at Potiphar's house and the wrongful imprisonment put him in position to interpret the dreams of the chief butler and chief baker. The two-year abandonment in prison paved the way for God's appointed time of Pharaoh's dreams. The chief butler remembering Joseph's interpretation of his dreams put him before Pharaoh and subsequent appointment as governor of Egypt. Each trying episode was difficult, but Joseph trusted God even when the events happening in his life were not clear and made no sense. Each life event refined Joseph to the person that he needed to be at a time and place appointed by God. Joseph's purpose was clear as he explained to his brothers that God has placed him in Egypt in advance to preserve the future generations of a nation. The intent of his brothers was evil, but God meant it for the good.

I selected this biblical story because of the personalized focus on Joseph's journey from a young boy to adulthood. The quantity of the content in Genesis sends a powerful message to us on the value of his story and message to us of uncompromising commitment to God. God clearly focused on the total person, and I believe it relates well to the shape concept discussed earlier. The three factors that empowers enduring hope are evident throughout his story.

God is the object of our hope: At each life event, God was the object of Joseph's hope. Joseph kept God at the forefront in his response to Potiphar's wife, the time in prison, his response to Pharaoh and elevation to governor of Egypt. His focus was not on his ability or intellect, but God gave Pharaoh the interpretation of his dreams through Joseph, and it was God that gave Joseph the wisdom to oversee Egypt's response to the famine.

God is sovereign: When Joseph revealed his identity to his brothers, he acknowledged that it was God that sent him to Egypt before them to preserve life. It was by God's providence the events occurred according to His purpose to include each difficult moment that would not make sense by human standards. Jacob and the entire extended family moved to Egypt and stayed until the appointed time according to His will.

God is trustworthy: Joseph trusted God at every difficult juncture of his journey, or else, disillusionment would have consumed him and derailed the opportunities to move with God at His appointed time.

As I now move to concluding thoughts in the next segment, the shaping I have personally experienced over these twenty years has made me more determined to bring hope, healing, purpose, and personal relationships to Jesus Christ through teaching, counseling, and the preaching gifts that God has given me. The experience of losing our son Jay is a part of God's shaping and the package of the total person—my SHAPE. I tend to focus heavily on spiritual gifts and purpose because God has given us purpose to pursue until He says that it is done. The giftings are only useful to others when we use them for service. This is in no way minimize the significance and impact of personal loss in our lives, but at some juncture in this journey, we must trust God in His grace and mercy to help us move forward in life according to His purpose for us. In time God helps us to work through the hurt and the difficulties of loss. So my encouragement to you is remain hopeful and seek and allow God to shape you for his purpose and for His glory.

Conclusion

As I started writing this book, I did not realize the journey it would take me on. My intent was simply to express that we can have enduring hope even in the midst of difficult times in life. I was amazed how God has kept us in the most strenuous times and my desire is to share what He has done. I had concerns of reliving the event of loss, and frankly, there were moments when I did, but at the same time, when I began exploring the Word of God and putting the factors together, it was His word that came alive. The factors are evident in His eternal Word and certainly not my own invention. They are who He is—God is the object of our hope, God is sovereign, and God is trustworthy. I pray that these truths and life application will bring hope to those who read this book. As I reflect on the chapters, I am ever grateful for the bases of our hope. When we feel the burden of loss and our hope is weak, there is a foundation that is strong and firm that we can stand. This is not on our own strength, but on His. For His word tells us, "The Lord is the strength of my life." In my personal experience of "faith on thin ice" moments, God assured me that He was with me when my faith was about to fail and could not see the next step in front of me. Even when our faith is moment by moment and day by day, God assures us that He is ever-present and reminds us in His word to stay close to Him because of His promise to never leave us alone.

When God answers our prayers, we come to the realization of putting our faith to work according to his eternal truth. I reflected on Psalm 91, which is a beautiful picture of God's promise of protection. As I wrote on this psalm, it was my intent to reflect on the process that Jay and I had memorizing this psalm together and our experience. I believe God confirmed for me that He was Jay's refuge in the combat zone and his protector. His soul is secure in the arms of Jesus Christ. But the Holy Spirit took me on an additional path that was a short focus on my young life. He reminded me that God was also my refuge and protector when Satan tried to take my life as a young fifteen-year-old in the streets of north Philadelphia. He also reminded me of the power of forgiveness for those who tried to take my life some nine years later as a young adult. The reflection of Psalm 91 was strengthening to me, and by God's grace and mercy toward us, we are assured that we can move forward in this life journey.

Every chapter was a direct impact on my journey. In the "Battles Within," I wrote about the two veterans I met who were struggling with loss and guilt. This made me more determined to present a message of hope and my prayer a practical guide to help them in their life struggles and for us to never forget what they have done for us. The experience in writing concludes at the last chapter, "The Shaping of Purpose," and the fascinating story of Joseph in the Old Testament. He was a man who had great trust in God at every difficult episode of his life. At first glance, the harshness of his brother's treatment of him by being sold in slavery and subsequent experiences would seem unfair, but he prevailed through his trust and great integrity and allowed God to shape him according to His sovereign plan and purpose. I found the story of Joseph to be a great biblical example of being shaped for God's purpose through trials, difficult circumstances, and moments of triumphs. He shapes us. This was a powerful reminder that the answers to our questions as to why difficult experiences happen may not come, but that we continue to trust God in His sovereignty in shaping us.

I firmly believe that the factors examined in this book and their life application empowers enduring hope for us. There is one final point to make for what empowers enduring hope. When I was describing the three factors that empowers enduring hope to a dear friend, mentor and colleague, Dr. William Scott, former director of the Triangle Bible Institute in Triangle, Virginia, where I currently teach, he listened very intently and reminded me of a critical point. Dr. Scott said that "enduring hope is also eternal." It was my hope to consult him on guidance for publishing and any other final considerations as I was finishing the last chapter, but Dr. Scott passed away two weeks after our discussion. From the eternal promise of God's word, Dr. Scott has gone home to be with the Lord! It is, therefore, appropriate for him to make the final critical point in this book. Several times I mentioned that for us to realize and experience enduring hope that's empowered by the three factors—God is the object of our hope, God is sovereign, and God is trustworthy—there must be a relationship with Jesus Christ for this to make sense. Dr. Scott's final point that enduring hope is also eternal is only made possible through our Lord and Savior Jesus Christ.

We have a choice to choose eternal hope in Jesus Christ or reject Him and face eternal damnation and separation from God. The Bible made this simple for us: "That if you confess with your mouth the Lord Jesus and believe in your heart that God has raised Him from the dead, you will be saved." It is just that simple. There is no let me get myself together first, or I am just too messed up. We were all born in sin and shaped into iniquity. You cannot get any worse in condition than the thief that was on a cross next to Jesus as He was being crucified. The thief recognized and believed who Jesus was and said to Him "Lord, remember me when you come into Your kingdom. And Jesus said to him, assuredly, I say to you, today you will be with Me in paradise." There was no time for that thief to get himself together before surrendering his life to Jesus Christ. So it is with you, come as you are and give your life to Jesus Christ with a sincere heart and experience the enduring and eternal hope that He promised us. May God bless you richly.

Bibliography

Bauer, Walter. *A Greek-English Lexicon of the New Testament and Other Early Christian Literature*. The University of Chicago Press, 1979.

Bromiley, Geoffrey W., ed. *The International Standard Bible Encyclopedia*. Vol. 1, A–D. William B. Eerdmans Publishing Co., 1979.

Dobson, James, C. *When God Doesn't Make Sense*. Tyndale House Publishers, Inc, 1993.

Foulkes, Frances. *Ephesians: An Introduction and Commentary*. Vol. 10. Tyndale New Testament Commentaries, InterVarsity Press, 1989.

Gonzalez, Guillermo, and Jay W. Richards. *The Privileged Planet*. Washington, DC: Regnery Publishing, 2004.

Lockyer, Herbert Sr., et al., eds. *Nelson's Illustrated Bible Dictionary*. Nashville: Thomas Nelson Publishers, 1986.

Patton, John. *Pastoral Care: An Essential Guide*. Nashville: Abingdon Press, 2005.

Pfeiffer, Charles F., Howard F. Vos, and John Rea, eds. *Wycliffe Bible Dictionary* Peabody, Massachusetts: Hendrickson Publishers, Inc., 2005.

Sproul, R. C., and Greg Bailey. *What Is Faith? Crucial Questions Book 8*. Grand Rapids: Reformation Trust, 2010.

Story, J. Lyle. *Jesus and the Issue of Suffering*. Virginia Beach: Regent University, 2008.

Swindoll, Charles R. *Joseph: A Man of Integrity and Forgiveness*. Nashville: Word Publishing, 1998.

Teal, Rodney A. *Reflections on Praise and Worship from a Biblical Perspective*. 2005. www.revrodneyteal.org.

Thiessen, Henry C. *Lectures in Systematic Theology*. Grand Rapids: William B. Eerdmans Publishing Company, 1997.

Warren, Rick. *The Purpose Driven Life: What on Earth Am I Here For?* Grand Rapids: Zondervan, 2012.

Websters Ninth New Collegiate Dictionary. Springfield, Massachusetts: Merriam-Webster Inc.

Willis, Avery T. Jr. *Master Life: Developing a Rich Personal Relationship with the Master*. Nashville: Broadman & Holman Publisher, 1998.

Vine, W. E., Merrill F. Unger, and William White. *Vine's Complete Expository Dictionary of Old and New Testament Words*. Thomas Nelson Publishers, 1996.

About the Author

Jack Bryant is a native of Philadelphia, Pennsylvania. In his early education, he has earned a bachelor of fine art degree from Temple University, Philadelphia, Pennsylvania, with a professional teaching certificate. He is an ordained minister serving his church as the assistant to the pastor and Christian Education director for the Star 
Bethlehem Missionary Baptist Church in Triangle, Virginia. For many years, he has been engaged in preaching, teaching biblical studies, facilitating seminars and the administration of Christian education programs for the church and community. He serves as faculty member and academic dean for the Triangle Bible Institute, Triangle, Virginia. He has a master of arts in practical theology from Regent University, Virginia Beach, Virginia.

Jack Bryant is an army veteran and retired career telecommunications manager with the Department of Defense. In this vocation, he has also earned a master of science in administration from Central Michigan University, Mt. Pleasant, Michigan, and master of arts in telecommunications from George Mason University, Fairfax, Virginia.

Jack and his wife Linda enjoy life together traveling and having fun with their two adult daughters and six grandchildren.